Secret

Shack

Don't judge Me

Gracelyn Love

Copyright

Dedication

~This book is dedicated to my beautiful, intelligent, and loving daughters, Katrina and Kristie,
whom I love dearly. In spite, of all my trials and tribulations, they continued to love and honor

me with respect and loyalty.~

~To my loving grandson Austin, for whom I hope this book will help him to better know and understand his grandmother.~
~To my beloved parents Grayson and Maggie (May), who loved and supported me throughout my ordeals.~
~To my blessed grandmother Louise (Ma), who prayed continuously during my troubles and hardships.~

Acknowledgements

I have to start by thanking Mrs. Letitia Washington, renowned author and writing coach, who looked at my manuscript and with her creative eye and writing experience suggested creating a realistic novel.
I must thank Mrs. Kelly Martin, book designer, who did not give up, on designing a powerful book cover based on my vision. She was determined to bring my vision to fruition.
Special thanks to my beta readers who did not hesitate to take on the reading of my manuscript. In return, they gave me many constructive criticisms, some of which I applied to my story.
Thank you, Mrs. Gail Williams, Mr. Mackie Williams, Elder Ruth Ann Lambe and
Reverend Maybelle Denwiddie.
Hallelujah! Thank you God for your love, grace and mercy.

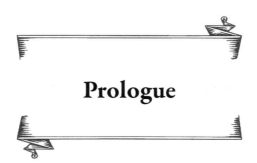

Prologue

I eased my car tires along the curb and cut off the engine. I was in a strange neighborhood on the other side of town, and had to admit, the area was pretty nice. A smattering of houses, prefaced with manicured lawns and proverbial white fences lined the street. Cutting the lights from the car, the only illumination came from the lampposts stationed on the sidewalk.

And the moon.

I slid down in my seat, hands still on the steering wheel, shaking like leaves fluttering in a breeze. I looked at them, and balled them into tight fists, but even that didn't make them stop.

Never would I have thought I'd be doing something like this. Never had I considered that I'd be back here, dealing with another man who had vowed to love and to cherish me, yet...

My blaring cell phone sliced into my anguished thoughts. The trill was so loud, I was certain it would wake up the entire neighborhood and alert the object of my investigation to my presence.

I shot my arm over to the passenger's seat and fished my phone out of my purse. "Lord help me," I muttered. Finally, I gripped and silenced it. Quickly, I took note of the number on the small screen. It was the private investigator, Ralph. I pressed the phone against my ear. "Hi, Ralph."

"Gracelyn, hello. I was just checking up on you to see if – "

I cut him off. "Yes, I found it," I answered. For the first time since parking, I scanned the houses in earnest. It was well past midnight, and many of the dwellings sat still and in darkness.

But there was one...

My eyes narrowed, just as an intense stinging burned the back of my eyes.

Yes, Ralph, I thought to myself. *I have found it.*

It was a green car, and *it* was parked in the back of the apartment building, next to a large, green garbage container, as if it belonged there. I'd snuck around the back of the residence, and that was when I'd seen it. Now, my eyes zipped to the house in question. The other houses were in complete darkness, but this one was lit up like a Christmas Tree.

My jaw tightened. "I've been sitting out here for almost an hour," I muttered. "It's well past midnight. I can't believe my husband would leave me alone at home for so long. He said he was out with friends. He said he'd be home. I can't believe he would – "

Ralph interrupted me. "This is a terrible situation," he said, as if confirming my innermost thoughts, "but the best thing you can do right now is to stay calm. I know you said you wanted to see it for yourself, but it would not be wise to overreact."

"Yes," I mumbled, but I didn't agree with him.

Ralph continued. "You've been collecting evidence for months, and finally, it has come down to this." He fell silent, as if waiting for me to say something, but the truth was, there was nothing I could say.

A small part of me wanted to believe that it wasn't true. Maybe this wasn't my husband's car, in this strange neighborhood, parked outside of this strange house on the other side of town. Maybe Ralph had been wrong when he reported having seen my husband in the company of another woman. There were tons of men who looked like Leopold. Could it be possible that Ralph had tracked and followed the wrong guy?

I had been through this before –twice before, if I am being precise. How could I have allowed it to happen again?

Suddenly, there was movement against the backdrop of the curtained window. Two silhouettes glided across like apparitions, but suddenly, they stopped. That was when I saw small arms reach up and thread around a neck; and a slender frame – one which looked entirely familiar – bent down. The ghostly shadows connected, in what I could only imagine, was a kiss.

A jolt rocked my body.

Ralph's advice, that I should stay calm, filtered through my head like a gust of wind in the treetops.

"Ralph, I have to go," I announced. Without waiting for a response, I slammed my finger on the button to disconnect the call and glared in the direction of the quaint home. The silhouettes had relocated, and now the front door was pushing open.

I plastered my body against the car seat, trying my best not to leap through the car window, but when my eyes took in the appalling sight before me, staying calm and keeping quiet was the last thing on my mind.

Chapter One
A Good Girl

"Gracelyn Love, are you ready for church?"

The bass in my father's voice cut through the walls to reach me all the way in my bedroom.

"Yes, I'm ready," I called back. I ran my hands over the light blue crinoline dress I'd chosen to wear this Sunday, and let my eyes fall to my shiny, black, patent leather shoes. About thirty minutes ago, Mama had pulled my hair into two tight ponytails, tied with light blue bows; and, thanks to the Vaseline, my face now rivaled the glow of the light burning in the bulb above my head.

I was a good girl, which meant that I was always ready, especially for church. Heavens, I'd only been going since before I was born, and that was eleven years ago. It was the expectation, and it would be the same for my three-year-old sister, Emily.

As if on cue, Emily released an ear-splitting yell. That sound was immediately followed by the scampering of Mama and Daddy's feet, as they rushed to her aid.

"Okay, Em," I heard Mama coo and coddle.

Daddy joined in. "I will get you some juice and snacks. Everything is going to be just fine. There's no need for the temper tantrum."

The wailing stopped, but my shoulders slumped.

My, how things had changed since Emily was born. For eight years, it had been just me, Mama, and Daddy. My thoughts traveled to our trips to the ice cream shop, which had always been the highlight of my week. It was never on the same day, because during the day, Daddy was a shoemaker. He also worked a lot as a taxi driver and chef, and we never knew when his early night off would be. Daddy, Mama, and I would pile into the car and take a long, unhurried drive to the U.S.A. Naval Base, which was located at the very east end of the island. That was where the ice cream shop was. Mama and I would always get vanilla on a cone, and Daddy would call us boring, especially with his adventurous, mint chocolate chip.

But when Emily was born, our family ritual changed. Sometimes, we'd go for weeks without taking our drive to get ice cream, and all of the special time that Mama and Daddy used to spend with me, was cut in half.

Emily needed a lot of attention, Mama said; but she didn't have to tell me anything. Surely, I could see it with my own two eyes.

A few minutes passed before we were heading for the car, Mama rocking my agitated sister on her hip.

Emily had really fair skin, compared to my darker hue, and now her face was flushed, eyes glassy. All that crying had really taken its toll.

"Okay, Em," Mama said, setting Emily's feet on the grass. "We're getting in the car now, so we can head to church. You like church, don't you?"

Emily huffed and pouted.

I should talk to her, I thought to myself – offer some sisterly advice and try to build our bond. I should tell her that Jesus doesn't like it when little girls, like us, misbehave.

Mama opened the back door for us, before climbing into her position next to Daddy, in the front.

I crouched down, close to Emily, determined to have an age-appropriate word with her, but Mama interrupted.

"Gracelyn, please help your sister into the back seat."

I paused and Emily scowled, just before ripping away and jumping into the back.

I'll talk to her later, I decided. *She's not in a good mood right now anyway.*

The drive to church wasn't a long one. In fact, the sanctuary was only five minutes away. Despite this, Daddy still found time to squeeze in a conversation with me.

"Summer is winding down, Gracelyn," he noted, catching my gaze in the rearview mirror before quickly returning his attention to the narrow, winding roads. "Are you ready to start your classes at The Berkeley Institute? It's a very prestigious school, you know. It carries a legacy of great men and women of color; men and women who have made local and global impacts."

"Yes," Mama agreed, twisting in the seat to peer at me. "And you've secured an educational scholarship, so we expect you to perform well academically and be on your best behavior."

I was fully aware of everything my parents had said and was about to tell them that I was more than ready to go to high school. My mind wandered to my time at Francis Patton School. It hadn't been a bad time. No, not at all. I had been a good student, well behaved, just as my parents required, with very good grades. I had always been conscious of my deportment at school. There was no way I could embarrass my parents by bringing home a poor report card, or by getting called into the principal's office.

Heavens no!

My parents were very strict, and there'd be no telling the punishment I'd receive if any of these things happened.

Francis Patton days had been okay; but there was one teacher I hadn't liked very much at all. It was Mrs. Jones, the lady who would rap the students' knuckles if they dared answer a question incorrectly. It never happened to me – but there *was* the time she'd marked my English paper, and that memory was etched into my mind. I'd never forget the way she'd called me to her desk, peering over those wire-rimmed glasses, that always seemed to sit perfectly on the tip of her nose. Her arm was outstretched, and between her fingers, was my English assignment.

"Miss Love, this is not your best work," she stated. Her tone sent a shiver racing up my spine, and instantly, my eyes burned.

I tried to straighten my shoulders – lift my chin – but she hadn't finished her assessment.

"This is very poorly written," she claimed. "It is almost as if a child from Greece has composed this story." She thrust her arm forward, as if it were not already fully extended.

That was when I saw my submission. It was emblazoned with red Xs, and large circles encased several words and sentences. The first of many tears fell, even as I shuffled my way back to my seat and laid my head on my desk, sobbing silently. It was on that day that I determined to improve my writing skills. Poetry and prose were my outlet in expressing my feelings and observations.

Yes, I was ready for high school, I thought, thinking about my father's question; even if it was just to get away from mean-old Mrs. Jones.

Now at church, daddy parked his car in the spot, where he always parked. No, it wasn't *his* spot, but because he was such a faithful member; and because he attended every service and supported every event, everyone simply knew that this spot belonged to Gerald Love.

Wives in oversized hats, accompanied by husbands in crisp, Sunday suits, filed through the wooden double door.

Had I been a little older, I might have applied the term Sunday Best, to describe the way all the adults looked when they came to church; but I was only eleven years old and knew nothing of such colloquialisms. Still, everyone looked dapper, and it was because they wanted to give God their best.

We made our way to our normal seats, in the third row, and I slid into the pew, flanked by Mama and Daddy.

Mama sat Emily on the seat.

I inhaled. *3... 2...1...*

Emily's cries of objection rose. Quickly, Mama tended to her, but Daddy also joined in the pampering.

"Now, now, Emily," he cooed. He was trying to be stern, but the endearing twinkle in his eyes completely nullified his efforts. "You're such a pretty girl, with your lovely, curly hair and beautiful skin. Don't let a heap of fussing mess that up, now."

Emily settled, but only a little.

Meanwhile, I sat thinking about my own hair and my own skin. People always talked about how beautiful Emily was, but when it came to me...

I frowned.

Daddy bowed his head to pray, the way he always did when we first entered the sanctuary. Mama followed suit, and the expectation was that I would do the same. I was a good girl, so of course I would.

I dipped my head and the two pony-tails mama had arranged fell forward.

What should I pray about, I wondered. I knew what Daddy was praying for. He was thanking God for bringing us through another week, and for his ability to provide for his family. He was also thanking God for Mama, Emily, and me.

Mama was thanking God for Daddy, because he was such a loving husband, a great father, and an excellent provider. She was thanking God for her two daughters as well.

Emily was still pouting, so I knew she wasn't thanking God for anything just then.

I clasped my hands and squeezed my eyes shut. "Lord, thank you for my mama, and my daddy, and even Emily – even though we don't really get along right now. Thank you for bringing us into your house every Wednesday and Sunday, so we can give your name praise. Thank you for helping me to be a good girl every day, and for helping me to do the right thing, even though it is difficult sometimes." I clasped my hands tighter and paused, thinking about what I had prayed for so far.

Was there something I was missing? Had I forgotten to ask God for something?

"Thank you for everything. Amen."

Diary Entry #1 Date: February 6, 1957

THE PROPER WAY

I've always crossed my T's
And dotted my I's
The Proper Way
I always said please and thank you
The Proper Way
May I, if you please
The Proper Way
Called when late
Jumped when asked
The Proper Way

Chapter Two
Too Many Rules

"Gracelyn, you coming or what?"

A group of friends peered at me, eyes twinkling with both excitement and mischief.

"If we're going to skip class to get taffy from the Candy Lady who lives up the hill, we need to go now!"

The offer was tempting. Not only did the lady up the hill sell taffy, she also had a delectable selection of glass candy. It came in all manner of colors and reminded me of a beautiful and tasty rainbow, but I was a good girl, which meant I'd never skip class. I could only imagine what my parents would do if a report indicating such ever got back to them.

My friends did this often – but not too often. The last thing any of us wanted was for the headmaster to find out about our shenanigans. Well, maybe I should speak for myself. If it was discovered that I was skipping the first part of French class to get treats off campus, it would mean a definite phone call to my mama and daddy – and because of how strict they were, them being called was definitely *not* an option.

Still...

The thought of that sticky taffy and colorful candy had me throwing caution to the wind.

"You all know I can't go," I reminded them, "but if I give you some money, you can get me my favorite candy."

"What do you want?" one of my friends asked.

My mouth watered, just thinking about the Candy Lady's delectable offerings. "One piece of taffy and one piece of glass candy," I informed my friend.

Before I knew it, my friends were returning just in time for the start of class, and I grinned when one of them handed me a brown paper bag full of goodies.

The French class was rambunctious. A bunch of boys were in the corner, making jokes and cackling like hyenas, while a group of girls were discussing the latest hairstyles, like the French Roll and the proper use of a hot comb.

Just then, Mr. Francis, the headmaster, slammed opened the door, face flustered. "You children – if you continue in this manner, not tending to your studies or paying attention in class – you will never be prepared to contribute to society in a meaningful way," he shouted.

But no one was fazed.

I slid into my seat, glad that the unruly class had disguised my friends' tardiness.

We were in our last year of high school and would be heading off to college in the fall. Just thinking about it sent a wave of excitement crashing over me. Oh, how I looked forward to escaping the confines of Bermuda and the expectations of the adults in my life. There were just so many rules to follow, to observe, and now that I was seventeen years old, I was growing tired of them. I wasn't little Gracelyn anymore. I was still a good girl, but to be honest, sometimes the pressure was too great.

I could never go to my friends' houses for birthday parties or sleepovers – Mama and Daddy weren't having that! I wasn't allowed to go to the movies or listen to *worldly* music. In fact, the only time I got an opportunity to hear the latest jams, like The Twist, was at school, when my friends would sing them during homeroom.

And don't even ask about dancing – no way! And with a boy? I wouldn't even let the thought enter my mind, lest Mama or Daddy somehow hear it.

No pants. No jeans. No jewelry. No makeup; and did I mention, no boys?

No. No. No.

Not only did my parents forbid these items and experiences, so did my Christian Brethren faith, the one I'd been born and raised in, and to make matters worse, at least six of my teachers attended my church. One was my Sunday School teacher for the teenagers' group. Another was an elder of the church, and four other teachers sat in the pew right across from me, every Sunday. Heavens, even the headmaster, was a tithe-paying member.

This all boiled down to one thing: all eyes on Gracelyn. There was never a break. The only time I could be myself – whatever that meant, was when I was laughing and talking with my friends at school. I was sick of it, ready for a change. I was ready to be unshackled from the expectations and the rules.

Only a few more months of this, I thought to myself, *then the shackles will be off.*

Chapter Three
Free At Last

D addy carried my luggage to the ticket counter and handed my passport to the gate agent, just as mama stepped up, holding a frowning Emily's hand. It was a bittersweet moment: *bitter* because I was about to leave the protection and shelter of my parents, yet *sweet*, for those very same reasons.

Both anticipation and anxiety flowed through my veins. I couldn't believe it. Finally, I was heading off to Ottawa, Canada, where I'd be studying to be a teacher, starting my life, embarking on a new journey – one which didn't require the scrutinizing eyes of adults.

I was a good girl, so of course there'd be a ton of studying and paying attention in my classes. I'd even be going to church, and continuing to worship as I had been taught; yet I would be a liar if I said the thought of being on my own didn't intrigue me.

Finally, I was all checked in. I threw my arms around Daddy's neck and squeezed him, trying to swallow back the tears crowding in my chest.

He reciprocated the display of affection and pressed a kiss on my forehead. Then, he pulled away and took me by the shoulders. "Now you go out there and make us proud, okay? You study hard and be a good girl. You know the way you've been raised," he reminded me. "Don't forget God. He will always direct your path, when you don't know what to do."

I nodded.

Mama chimed in. "And make sure to call us as soon as you arrive and get settled, and then once a week after that," she stipulated. "We'll need to know how your classes are going." She thought of something else. "And choose your friends wisely. If they aren't God-fearing young ladies, they won't make good friends."

Again, I nodded.

It was time to head off. I glanced at Emily. I still hadn't had that sisterly-talk with her, but that wasn't because I hadn't tried. I'd attempted to connect with her on several occasions, especially now that we were getting older, but for some reason, there was a chasm between us. Over the years, a wedge had inserted itself into our relationship, and though I'd tried to bridge the gap, I'd been unsuccessful.

I pasted a smile onto my face. "I guess I'll see you later too," I offered. "When I call home, I'll ask to speak to you. Then we can talk and – "

"I won't want to talk," she interrupted.

My mouth snapped shut.

THE SILVER BIRD LIFTED into the sky and I pressed my forehead against the small window, watching as the pastel-colored houses, with the white roofs, diminished and disappeared beneath a thick band of clouds.

I sat back and closed my eyes.

Free. Free at last, I thought to myself.

Now, it was *really* just me. No Mama, no Daddy, and no Emily. Just my matching red luggage and me, dressed in a green suit, matching green hat, with heels and gloves, as if I were going to church.

Thank God, Free at last!

IT WAS LATE AT NIGHT when my taxi finally rolled through, what was about to be, my new neighborhood. It was early September, so there wasn't any snow yet; but the temperature was so cold, I was certain it would only be a matter of time before those white flakes dusted the ground.

The taxi driver pulled up in front of a two-story apartment building, which was buzzing with life, despite the hour.

I pulled at the scarf around my neck, just as two girls appeared on the stoop.

"Nancy! Cheryl, come quickly! She's here!"

It was cold outside, but the reception from these girls warmed me to the bone. In an instant, three others peeked outside of the door, and then, in one swift move, they bounded off the steps.

"Gracelyn Love!"

"Yes, that's me," I confirmed. The smile on my face stretched my cheeks and made them hurt.

Without warning, I was pulled into a girly group hug.

"We are so excited to have you as our new roommate," the first girl squealed. "My name is Joan, and this is Sharon." She restated the names of the others, even though I'd heard her belt out their names from the stoop.

My new roommates grabbed pieces of my luggage and dragged them into the apartment. As soon as the door opened wider, the sound of music – *worldly* music – filled my ears, and I was surprised to find the place teeming with people – both girls and... boys.

I advanced deeper into the apartment building, and my eyes turned towards the open door of the lower apartment, which was crowded with young people. They were dancing, laughing and having a blast! The record player blared, pumping out loud music, and I couldn't help but sway my hips to the thumping beat of the music.

No Mama, no Daddy! No Mama, no Daddy!

These words ran through my mind in tune with the beat.

That was when I noticed a white guy sitting in the corner of the living room amongst a group of friends. And that was also when I noticed that *he* was noticing *me* too.

His blue eyes seemed to be the same color as the pristine island waters I'd just left behind, and when he smiled at me, I gasped and jerked my gaze away.

I cleared my throat. "Is it always this... busy around here?" I asked Cheryl, but I didn't really care about her answer.

We started to ascend a flight of stairs to my apartment. Cheryl opened the door and we headed down the hall, to where I assumed was my bedroom; but secretly, I wished that I could have stolen another peek at Mr. Blue Eyes.

"Only on weekends," Cheryl answered the question I'd forgotten I even asked. "We know how to have fun around here, but make no mistake, our studies are very important. Secretly, we're nerds." She pressed her index finger against her lipstick adorned mouth. "But don't tell anyone," she warned. "We have a reputation to maintain."

We burst into a fit of laughter.

I spent the next couple of hours organizing my room, and my five new roommates assisted. After most of my things had been packed away, I decided it was time to get some rest. It had been a long, emotional day, and the traveling was starting to take its toll.

So were thoughts of Mr. Blue Eyes.

I picked up the phone and connected to the operator. Then, I waited for Daddy to answer. The minute his voice hit my ear drum; I felt a surge of rejuvenation.

"Daddy, I'm here in Ottawa," I informed him. "I arrived safely."

"Oh, Gracelyn, that's wonderful. I'm so glad you called, like we asked. Your mother and I were starting to get worried."

My mouth pinched.

Shackles...

"There was no need to worry, Daddy," I assured him. "It took a while to get from the airport to my new apartment. And then, I decided to unpack a few things before I settled down and gave you a call."

"I understand," he said.

I exhaled a sigh of relief.

My mama grabbed the phone. "Gracelyn, is everything all right?"

"Everything is great," I responded, feeling my shoulders wither some more.

"Have you met your roommates yet? Are they God-fearing girls, like you?"

"They're wonderful," I answered, being careful not to discuss the status of their salvation. "We're going to get along well. In fact, one of the girls, Sharon, is going to teach me how to make spaghetti from scratch!"

"Gracelyn, that sounds wonderful," Mama said, and then she paused. "What's that noise?"

My body jerked at the question. "What noise, mama?"

"That noise," she said again, but this time, her voice had lost the exuberance that had been in it, and now it sounded strained. Agitated. "It sounds like music," she clarified. "And people. Gracelyn Love, are you at a party?"

I eased my way to the door and slid it closed.

Now, Daddy was on the line. "Gracelyn?"

"No, I'm not at a party," I insisted. "I've just arrived in Ottawa, how could it even be possible?" I asked. "What you hear is the television. The walls are thin and my roommate is watching a television program in the bedroom next to mine."

Silence fell over the connection. It was the kind of silence which implied skepticism.

"Okay well..." Daddy inhaled. "As I said, you just make sure to stick with your morals and your values. You're a good girl," he reminded me, and I silently mouthed the last part of the sentence with him. "No worldly music, no worldly television shows, no parties, and definitely no boys."

I frowned, but remained silent, allowing my daddy to think his reminders were sinking in, but the truth was, they were going through one ear and out the other.

"Daddy," I finally said.

"Yes, sweetheart?"

I paused. I was trying to consider how many ways there were for me to ask him the next questions, but when I couldn't think of many, I decided to come right out. "When do you think I'll be ready to actually date a guy?"

Daddy almost gasped. "Well, certainly not any time soon," was his immediate answer. "You're only eighteen, and right now you need to focus on your studies."

Mama was saying something in the background, but Daddy quieted her.

"Perhaps when you're in your mid-twenties," he suggested.

I ended the phone call after a few more excruciating minutes. The content of the conversation was troubling. The shackles, they were trying to fit themselves back onto my ankles; but now, I was miles away from home, which meant I didn't have to do everything my parents said anymore. It didn't mean I wouldn't do some things. Just not everything.

And they would never know.

I'd keep it all a secret.

What my parents didn't know wouldn't hurt them, that's how the saying went, anyway.

With that satisfying thought, I finally drifted off into a content sleep, excited about what the following days would bring.

Chapter Four
College Life

It didn't take long for me to become acclimated to the college lifestyle. In fact, by week four, I'd traded the stocking, heels, and gloves I'd been wearing in the airport, for dungarees, sneakers, and candy-apple nail lacquer. The freedom, the one I'd been dreaming about for as long as I could remember, had finally come. I'd call my parents every Sunday night, and each time, my father would ask me the same questions:

"Gracelyn Love, did you get in early and go to church today?"

"Of course, Daddy," would be my quick response. "I got in very early." *Like, five o'clock in the morning early...* "and I attended the worship service."

Immediately, I'd hear the smile in his voice. "Wonderful. You're such a good girl, Gracelyn, and you're making your mother and I very proud."

I'd smile, satisfied that I hadn't lied to my daddy.

Well, not completely.

And besides, it was just as I'd decided four weeks ago: what my parents didn't know wouldn't hurt them; and that included the parties I attended and the road trip I took across the province boundary with my roommates. A prime example was the one occasion during which we jumped into Cheryl's car and crossed over to Hull, which was in Quebec. We had a blast, until it was time to return.

"Ma'am, your identification, please?"

Cheryl blinked a few times before reaching into her purse and pulling out her drivers' license.

Something didn't feel right about this. We were not accustomed to taking trips on weekends. But we were adventurous, this weekend. Therefore, we'd all pile into Cheryl's car and whizz off, making sure to return in enough time to get some rest. After all, there were classes to attend on Monday morning, and I was still attending church services, every now and then.

Cheryl sat in the front, offering her sweetest smile to the staunch border patrol man. Meanwhile the rest of us sat in the back, not daring to make a peep. In fact, my heart was thumping so wildly in my chest, I was certain that it would only be a matter of minutes before it came flying out and landed on the ground.

The border patrol man regarded the ID for a few seconds, before shaking his head and conferring with his partner. Suddenly, he pinned us with severe eyes. "Ladies, what business do you have in Ottawa?"

"Oh, we're students at Ottawa Teachers' College," Cheryl answered quickly. "We're about to finish up our semester there."

The man's eyes narrowed. "Are you Canadian?"

"No sir," I answered. "We're from Bermuda."

"Do you mean Jamaica?" he asked, as if I didn't know what country I was from.

My teeth clamped, but I tried to relax my jaw. "No sir, Bermuda," I clarified, keeping my tone light.

Cheryl chimed in. "It's an island, like Jamaica is, but it's about two hours away from Boston and New York City."

We waited for the patrolman to smile and bob his head in remembrance. We were used to scenarios like this. In fact, it seemed as if many Canadians had not been exposed to people of African descent. Because of this, we were always educating about our culture and where we were from.

But the patrolman's frown only deepened. A piercing beep, and the sound of a staticky voice coming over a walkie-talkie disguised his communication with his colleague.

"Ladies, we're gonna have to verify your identities before we can let you cross this here border."

"What?" I shrieked.

"We advise you to be patient," the other man suggested; but he wasn't fooling me. It wasn't a suggestion at all. It was a command.

My mind started going faster than Cheryl's car had ever gone. Thoughts of what my father and mother would say – and do – blitzed my mind. If Daddy ever found out about this one secret, it could potentially mean that all the other secrets I'd kept would spill out; like the fact that I wasn't going to church as frequently as he thought I was; or the fact that I was attending parties and listening to worldly music, and talking to young men...

If Daddy ever found out about this, he would kill me! Not literally, but the shame I'd feel, I would wish I was dead.

There was no way I could not get across this border. There was no way I could not get back to campus. There was just no way.

Hours passed, and by now, the make-up Cheryl had taught me how to wear looked like a paint job gone wrong on my face. And I wasn't the only one who was an emotional mess. All of my roommates had been reduced to blubbering fools.

I suggested we pray. No, I hadn't been going to church as frequently as I should have, but it was worth a shot.

The border patrol men had pulled out a thick, dusty, black book, and were scouring the pages, but suddenly, they looked up and called us over.

I smeared residue tears and snot over my face with the back of my hand, and approached the men, with the rest of my roommates.

"Ladies, we have some good news. We can confirm the existence of your country, as well as your status as enrolled students at Ottawa

Teachers' College." Despite the optimistic news, both men continued to glare at us.

We crumbled to our knees with relief, grateful that God had answered our prayer. Then we sped over the border, and I reminded Cheryl to observe the speed limit.

That was the last time we'd ventured across the boundary, but the weekends still transformed our apartment building into Party Central. To be clear, us girls were never the ones to host a party. Somehow, that didn't seem proper or fitting for young ladies, such as ourselves; however; the entire neighborhood could count on the boys living on the first floor to throw a bash – and of course, we girls would attend. Somehow it didn't seem proper or fitting not to, especially since they were our neighbors.

This weekend was no different. The bass from the music wafted up through the ceiling and settled on the soles of my feet, and I couldn't help but tap them to the mesmerizing beat of a popular song. I stood in front of the stove, stirring the spaghetti sauce bubbling in the pan. Simultaneously, the water in a large pot began to roll, and I tipped a box of pasta into it.

Sharon peered into the kitchen. "Gracelyn, how are you making out with that spaghetti? The boys are saying they're hungry and they're wondering what's taking you so long."

This weekend, I decided to make spaghetti for everyone. I'd made enough spaghetti to last a lifetime.

I smiled, twisting the spoon around the edge of the pot. "Please tell those greedy boys I'll be done soon," I requested, and as soon as she disappeared to pass on my message, I picked up the pace. I grabbed the ingredients that Cheryl had specified when she taught me how to make it the day after I'd arrived and added them to the bubbling sauce. Then, I stirred the pasta for a few seconds. Quickly, I plucked out a strand and prepared to throw it on the wall, just to see if it stuck. According to Cheryl, that's how I would know when it was ready.

With a quick toss, I flung the strand against the wall and beamed when it held. "Perfect!" I muttered.

"I have to admit, I agree," a deep voice added in corroboration.

I gasped and spun around so fast I almost burned my backside on the still-lit stove.

It was Mr. Blue Eyes.

Of course, by now I knew that his name was Jackson Reed. He was one of the boys who lived on the first floor, and he'd also been the one I'd seen that very first night, when I arrived. Ever since then, I hadn't been able to get those electric-blue eyes out of my mind. Even though a month had passed, I hadn't built up the courage to strike up a conversation with him, even though it was obvious he thought I was pretty.

That's what Cheryl told me anyway. She said a girl would always know when a young man liked them, because he would always stare, and his eyes would twinkle.

Well, if that was the case, there was no doubt that Jackson was interested, because his blue eyes gave him away every time.

But I had never talked to a young man like him in my life, let alone a white guy; and now, Jackson was standing in front of me, waiting for me to say something.

Silence.

Jackson jerked his hand forward. "Maybe I can help you with the spaghetti," he offered. "After all, we are waiting."

I laughed and so did he. "I wouldn't mind a little help," I considered finally turning off the stove. I gave the pasta a final stir and didn't even notice when Jackson snuck up behind me with a colander. Quickly, I collected myself. There was no way I could let Jackson know that I wasn't used to being this close to a guy.

"So... is it cold enough for you?"

"Oh, definitely yes," I informed him, chuckling. "In Bermuda, it gets cold during the winter, but certainly nothing like this; and neither does it snow, thanks to the Gulf Stream."

"Oh wow, I didn't realize that," Jackson admitted, quirking his eyebrows.

"And I had never seen snow, until I got here either."

Jackson smiled and rested his hand on my shoulder. Warmth from his hand seemed to penetrate the fabric of my shirt. "Then perhaps, tomorrow evening, we can explore this winter wonderland called Ottawa, together. For example, the Rideau Canal is within walking distance." Jackson shrugged a lazy shoulder. "Or maybe we can hop in my convertible and we can take a drive. Then, we can come back and get to know each other more over two mugs of hot cocoa."

"I'd like that," I agreed, through a girlish giggle. I didn't tell Jackson that my roommates and I had toured the surrounding area a million times by now. In fact, he probably already knew it, but neither of us would deny that it would be a lot more fun to do it together.

The next night, Jackson and I met up, as discussed; and after a few hours of driving, talking, and laughing, we returned home to the much-anticipated mug of cocoa. It was during that initial conversation that I learned more about him. He was five years older than me and had already graduated from the University of Cambridge in Ottawa. I told him about my experiences in Bermuda, as well as about a few of the adventures I'd had since being in Canada. To my content, we talked and laughed for hours.

It wasn't long before weeks transformed into months, and before I knew it, I was on the threshold of the completion of my first year at Ottawa Teachers' College. It had been hard work, but in reflection, I had no doubt that I'd adjust well. Not only had I adjusted, I'd successfully broken free from the bondage of expectation and rules that had been set for me all my life. Not only had I experienced a year away from my parents, I'd successfully navigated many situations on my own, including my first romantic relationship with Jackson. I had put away childish things, and now, I was living life on my own terms, the way a real woman should.

Jackson and I had been going steady since our initial meeting in the kitchen, and our romance had transformed and blossomed into a strong bond. We were inseparable. If I wasn't spending quality girl-time with my roommates, they all knew where they could find me. Jackson worked during the day, but in the evening, when I'd finished class, I'd go downstairs to his apartment and study, well, that is what I would tell my parents.

"Gracelyn, I can't believe that your first year is just about complete," he commented one evening. We were snuggled up in a blanket in each other's arms, on the couch. He had been whispering sweet nothings in my ear. I playfully, kept pushing him away. We spent several hours to-gether each evening, sharing our feelings and our day.

"I know," I agreed. "I guess the saying is true: time flies when you're having fun." I pulled my eyes up to his, but the bright smile and twin-kling blue eyes that always greeted me were not there. Instead, his mouth was creased with concern. I frowned and pushed the blanket aside. "Jackson, is everything okay? You don't seem happy with this conversation."

"I can't say that I am," he admitted through a sigh. He folded up the blanket and raked his hands through his blond hair. "The completion of your first year means there's only one year left for you to be in Cana-da; for us to be together," he clarified.

My mouth pinched.

"You have to return to Bermuda, don't you?"

"Yeah," I confirmed. "The terms of my bursary require that I return and teach for two years, after graduation." I picked up the blanket and placed it on the arm of the couch, rubbing the back of my neck. "But I guess I still don't understand," I admitted. "I would have thought you'd be happy to know that I'm graduating soon. You've been the one push-ing and encouraging me."

"Don't get me wrong, Gracelyn," he encouraged me, taking my hands into his, "I'm very happy and very proud of the fact that you'll be completing your studies. That's not the reason I'm upset," he said, shaking his head. "I guess what bothers me is the thought that when you graduate, you're going to leave me. There'll be no more us."

Instantly, my heart softened as I began to comprehend his trepidation. He hadn't been the only one thinking about the fact that when I left Canada, the likelihood of us ever seeing each other again would be drastically reduced. For almost an entire year, we'd been inseparable, and the reality was, in less than a year, it would all be coming to an end.

A sudden, heavy weight cloaked itself over my shoulders, and when I noticed the way Jackson's shoulders were slumped forward, it was obvious he was feeling the weight also.

My jaw trembled. "You know, I've never done a long-distance relationship before," I reminded him. "In fact, you're my first, true boyfriend, so I've never done anything other than us."

We burst into laughter, but after a second, Jackson settled.

"Gracelyn Love, this past year has been the best of my life. Spending time and getting to know you has been more than I ever dreamed it would be. I really wish our relationship didn't have to end."

"Me too," I agreed, trying to ignore the heat spreading across my cheeks.

"And I was thinking that maybe it doesn't have to."

Now, my heart hitched against my ribcage. "Jackson, what on earth are you talking about?" I said through a breath.

His eyes brightened, as if a marvelous idea had popped into his head. In fact, the look in his eyes was so intense, I could feel it piercing my soul. "Let's get married," he blurted.

I almost choked.

"I've been thinking about it, for a couple of weeks actually," Jackson continued, oblivious to my lack of oxygen. "After you graduate next year, let's do it. You've already met my parents, and they love you, like you were their own daughter!"

"I can't deny that," I admitted, considering his proposal in earnest.

"I can come to Bermuda and meet your parents," he suggested.

"Well, when would you do that?" I asked.

"I could do it whenever you like," he said quickly, "in fact, the sooner the better. I'd love to meet your parents."

I opened my mouth, wishing I could say something, but no words would come out. Was Jackson really serious right now? Did he really believe in our love? Did he really want to marry me?

Thoughts flew around my head like snow in a snowstorm, and when I jerked my stinging eyes back up to his questioning ones, his smile flickered.

"Do you... not want to get married?" he whispered. Hurt splashed across his face and he swallowed. "You love me just as much as I love you... don't you, Gracelyn?"

"Of course I do," I reassured him quickly. "And Jackson, of course I'll marry you! I would like nothing more than to be your wife."

The second year of college passed as quickly as the first, I made the decision to stay an additional year and take a course in Integrated Studies, and before I knew it, the reality of Jackson and I becoming husband and wife was beckoning. We'd been talking about it for two years now, but now it was time for me to return to Bermuda to render my service back to the Government teaching in the public school system.

I could still remember the moment I boarded that airplane and left Jackson waving goodbye, his blue eyes looking dull. I had traveled home over the breaks before, but surely, this would be different. Despite this, Jackson and I decided to try our hand at a long-distance relationship. The thought of not being together was something neither of us could fathom, and besides, we were getting married! As soon as my two years of teaching expired, I was going to pack my bags and move back to Ottawa to be with the love of my life. In the meantime, he'd visit Bermuda so that we could remain connected.

Three months after my return to Bermuda, Jackson was making preparations for his first trip. By now, I had opened up to my parents and told them about my relationship. It had been a tough conversation, but eventually, Daddy and Mama realized that I was a young woman and that I was ready to embark on the next phase of my life.

The night before, I barely slept a wink. I tossed and turned in my bed until finally I threw my feet over the edge and dropped my head into my hands. I glanced at the clock on the wall, shocked to see that it was just after midnight.

I dragged myself out of the bed and headed for the kitchen to get a drink of water. When I arrived, I was surprised to find my father already in there.

"Dad," I squeaked in shock. "What are you doing here?"

He held up his glass and smiled. "Couldn't sleep," he confessed. He opened the fridge and pulled out the pitcher. I watched as he poured water into an empty glass and then handed it to me.

I leaned on the counter next to him and pressed the glass against my bottom lip.

"Why aren't you asleep?" he asked. "You have an exciting day tomorrow. Jackson, the man you've told me so much about, will be here. I'll finally get to meet him."

"Maybe that's the reason I'm still up," I said, chuckling. "I'm a little bit nervous, Daddy."

"What would you be nervous about?" he asked, brows drawn in. "The two of you have been dating for a while, haven't you?"

"Yeah," I answered slowly, recognizing it for the trick question that it was, "but that's not what I mean." I pressed my mouth into a straight line and pulled my shoulders up to my ears. "I guess I'm a little nervous about him meeting you."

Daddy feigned shock and pressed his hand against his chest. "Am I not *cool* enough for your boyfriend?"

l was shocked that my daddy used the word *cool. He must have really been getting hip*, because I had never heard him talk like that in my life! I laughed and so did Daddy. "That's not what I meant either," I said, and then I settled. "I guess I'm a little worried about what will happen if you don't like him," I wondered. "I mean, Jackson is an awesome guy, and I don't think you'll not like him, but there's always a chance, you know?"

Daddy rested his glass on the counter and pulled me into an embrace. "Gracelyn Love, if you've chosen him to be your boyfriend, I'm sure he's a wonderful man. You're a good girl so I have no doubt you've chosen a suitable partner."

Daddy squeezed me and I smiled as he pressed a kiss on the top of my head.

"We're planning on getting married, you know," I mentioned. Before now, I hadn't said anything. In fact, there were a few things that Daddy and Mama didn't know, and I was very strategic about what I told them. I continued. "I'm a little concerned about the distance. When we were together every day, it was a lot easier; but now that we're not, it's harder."

Daddy's arms stiffened around me, but before I could really notice it, his muscles relaxed. "Long distance relationships can be a lot of work," he said, "but remember, God is in control of everything; and if it is meant to be, it will last."

Daddy was right that day. Jackson and I tried our hardest to make our relationship work, but it seemed as if time and distance ate away at the potency of our love. Our marriage never came to pass, but I would learn that nothing could take away our bond, because we remained friends forever.

Diary Entry #2 Date: January 4, 1965

<u>THE RIGHT MAN?</u>

Is there the Right Man?
No! There are two sides to every man
Right and Wrong
Accept the right
Wrong will follow
I want a total, good man
Accept the right,
Wrong
One can say,
Loudly.

Chapter Five
Garrett

One Year Later

"Mama, I'm home from work!" My voice rang out in the house, but there was no immediate answer. I pulled my purse from my shoulder and opened the fridge, trying to determine what might be prepared for supper. At the same time, my mind was filled with ideas for the lessons I would teach to my first-grade class in the morning. I was teaching them phonics and had developed several songs, which would help them to remember the letter sounds.

But that wasn't the only thing I had to think about. It was Wednesday, so that meant I would be required to attend mid-week prayer and there were several people on the prayer list. Then there was the Sunday School lesson I needed to start thinking about. Not only did I teach first graders at Francis Patton, I also taught them scripture lessons on Sundays.

I sighed.

This was my life.

By no means was it a bad life. I was a college-educated woman with a good job. Granted, I was living in my parents' house, sleeping in the same bed since I had been a child – but that was the expectation of young, unmarried women. To move out of the homestead and get a place on your own... well, any such girl would be sure to be the talk of the town.

And I was Gracelyn Love.

I was obedient and respectful.

I was courteous, polite and ladylike.

I was everything that my parents and everyone else expected me to be...

I sighed and my shoulders slumped forward as the cool air from the still-open fridge slammed into me.

Who was I trying to fool? After living on my own for two years; and after all of the adventures I'd experienced, my life had become boring! I was restless and antsy. I was simply going through the motions of completing the mundane tasks that comprised my everyday routine: school, church, home.

I ripped my mind off of these thoughts, the ones that sailed through my mind on a daily basis and focused my attention on what was in the fridge. When I noticed there was nothing interesting, even in there, I slammed it closed.

"Mama, I'm home!" I called out.

Still no answer.

I snatched an apple from the fruit bowl, and that was when I noticed a note sitting next to it on the counter:

Gracelyn, I've gone to work and will need to be picked up at four o'clock. I'll see you then, and thanks in advance. ~ Mama.

I glanced at my watch and took stock of the time. School got out at three o'clock, and by now, it was just after three thirty. I'd need to hurry if I was going to get to her job on time, especially if I wanted to abide by the speed limit.

I clamped the apple between my teeth, grabbed the car keys and headed out the door.

It took about twenty minutes to get from where I lived on Crawl Hill to Hamilton Princess Hotel, which was in the heart of the island, in the city. It was a luxurious hotel, one of the most expensive on the island. Whenever celebrities visited the island, this was one of the places they often stayed. Because of this, I wasn't surprised to see workmen stationed at various points on the perimeter of the hotel, painting the walls and tending to the foliage.

I maneuvered my parents' car into the busy parking lot and cut the engine, just as one man began to slap paint against a wall. The relentless late afternoon sun was beating against his brow, and he swiped his forearm over his head. There was no way I couldn't help but notice how attractive he was, and since I'd been on my own for three years, I had a little more experience dealing with the opposite sex. In fact, under Cheryl's tutelage, I was now very secure in my ability to start and hold a conversation with a man.

Quickly, I dug into the big canvas bag I took to class. Inside, it had all sorts of treats, goodies, and snacks for my students. When my hand closed around a thermos of water, I smiled to myself. Then, I took the keys out of the ignition and hopped out of the car. "I have a thermos of water, if you're thirsty," I called out making my way over to the hardworking man.

He looked up and squinted in my direction, and I held the thermos up. "You're right on time with that," he said, and the smile he donned was enough to compete with the setting sun.

"Perfect," I said. I rushed over, handed him the water, and watched as he took a hearty swig. His Adam's apple bobbed as he chugged the water back, and I smiled, happy to have done a good deed for someone in need, but happier that I was able to get a closer look at this man.

The handsome young man swiped his hand over the back of his mouth. "It's been a long day, and this was right on time," he confirmed. "I must say, I've never seen you before, and trust me, a pretty face like yours wouldn't go unnoticed by me."

"My mother works here, and she's about to knock off," I said. "I don't normally pick her up from work. In fact, I work at the other end of the island."

"Then that would explain why I'm just making your acquaintance."

We continued a meaningful conversation for a couple of minutes, and all too soon, my mother was rounding the corner. I waved to her and let her know I was on my way to the car. She frowned a little but got inside.

My belly churned. "My mama is here, so it looks like I have to go," I said, "but it was really good talking to you."

"Likewise," he agreed. "My name is Garrett," he said. "What's your name?"

"Gracelyn Love."

Garrett gasped. "Is that... really your name?"

"Gracelyn Love, will you hurry? It's been a long day and I'm ready to go home," my mama called out from the car.

"Well, I guess that answers my question," he considered as we laughed.

I offered him an apologetic glance, as I turned to hurry away. When I turned to look back at him, he was still staring at me.

"Will I see you tomorrow?" he called out?

I shrugged and disappeared inside of the car. The minute I closed the door, my mama grunted. "Well, who was that?" she bit out. It was obvious that she didn't like the look of Garrett, but it was also obvious that she had no good reason to come to any conclusions about him.

"His name is Garrett," I said, turning the key in the ignition. "And before you ask, no, I don't know him. In fact, I just met him, while I was waiting to pick you up." The skin on my cheeks warmed. "He seems like a really nice guy."

"Well, you don't know that," Mama barked. "And just in case you forgot, it's not nice for a young lady to be seen talking to a man on the side of the street, like she's some hussy!"

I drew in a breath. "Mama, you're being a little dramatic," I suggested easily. "For one, I wasn't on the side of the street. I was outside of your job, waiting for you to finish work."

She folded her arms over her chest and glared out of the window.

"Secondly," I continued gently, "we were only talking. He was working hard, and I had an extra thermos of water, that I thought to offer him. The way I see it, Jesus would have been really pleased with my act of kindness."

Hearing that, my mama's shoulders loosened a little, but I could tell my rebuttal hadn't been completely satisfactory.

The next day, before I left for work, I informed my mama that I would pick her up when she knocked off, the way I had the day before. The entire drive to Hamilton Princess, I prayed to God and asked Him to allow me to bump into Garrett. I didn't know whether my prayer was becoming of a Christian young lady, but when I arrived and Garrett was there, painting the very same wall, it was confirmation that God was pleased with my supplication.

Our *impromptu* meetings continued for the rest of the week, and well into the next one, and finally, Garrett asked me out on a date. I quickly explained to him that even though I was a grown woman of twenty-one years, I still lived under my parents' roof. Not only that, I honored and respected my parents' wishes, as a proper, Christian woman should. Because of this, going out on a date wasn't possible; however, if he wanted, he was more than welcome to come to my home, where we could watch television and talk.

Garrett observed me closely, and I waited, with bated breath, to hear what his response would be. Secretly, this was the part I had been dreading: telling him the truth about how severe my parents were. He'd already been subjected to my mama's glares every time I picked her up from work. Whenever he asked, I'd tell him she'd had a long day – and of course her commands to hurry up and get in the car because she was tired corroborated this claim. But now, I had put it all out there, and I was at his mercy, waiting to see if he would accept me for who I was.

Suddenly, Garrett smiled. "I'd love to come to your home and spend time with you," he whispered. His voice was like oozing honey. "I guess I'll see you tonight after I knock off and freshen up."

"That would be perfect!"

"GRACELYN LOVE, IT'S past midnight. It's time for your friend Garrett to leave."

Those were the words my father would mutter every night for the next two years as Garrett's and my friendship blossomed into a full romantic relationship. And every time, my body would tighten, and blood would rush into my cheeks.

"Yes, daddy," I'd respond, fighting the urge to look into Garrett's face.

My father would slink back down the hallway, leaving us alone.

I sighed as Garrett lifted himself off the couch and pulled me into his arms. Quickly, he'd scan the room, just to make sure neither of the keepers was present, and when the coast was clear, he'd press a tender kiss onto my lips. The urge to melt into his arms was one I was never able to fight. In fact, I'd given up fighting it a long time ago.

Garrett sighed. "This routine is getting old," he murmured, lips still pressed against mine.

"What routine is that?"

"The one where we say goodbye every night," he clarified.

I rested my head on his chest in silent agreement.

"Maybe we should change that..."

Now I jerked up to look into his face. "What are you talking about?"

Garrett's eyes fluttered and he stepped away, raking his hands over his close-cut hair. "I want you to be my wife, Gracelyn," he said. "I've been thinking about it for a long time. We've been dating for a while, and I'm certain, there's no other woman I'd rather be with."

I threw my hands over my mouth in shock. "Garrett, do you really mean that?"

"I do," he said with a firm nod. "So... will you marry me?"

The response was on the tip of my tongue. For a second, I thought about Jackson, and his promise of marriage, but the distance between us had been too much for us to survive.

This was different.

Garrett and I saw each other every day. There was no distance to test the strength of our love, and the way we felt for one another was undeniable.

I nodded, my hair bouncing around my ears, and a smile spread across my lips. "I will," I committed. "I will marry you."

Immediately, Garrett kissed my lips, and this time, if my parents had seen fit to venture down the hall, they would have been privy to everything. "You have made me the happiest man in the world," he alleged. "In the morning, I will speak with your father and get his permission. After that, you need to start planning. I want you to be my wife as soon as possible."

Several kisses later, Garrett was heading home, and I tossed and turned in my bed, thanks to my full heart, which was threatening to burst out of my chest.

Chapter Six
A Disturbing Telephone Call

Ten Years Later...

"**H**as Garrett's football game ended?" Daddy glanced at me over the meat and roasted potatoes mama had made for Sunday dinner, and then quickly looked back into his plate.

I adjusted my nine-year-old daughter's chair and reminded her to use her table etiquette when eating at the table, and quickly attended to the newest addition, who had just turned one year old. My father's question bothered me, but I couldn't let him see that.

He would worry, and the last thing I wanted was a worrying father.

Or mother. But the way Mama dissected her potatoes let me know she'd already passed that point.

"If it hasn't ended, it should be over shortly," I responded cutting into my own food. "This is normal. We've been married for ten years now, and he's always been big into football, you know that, Daddy."

Daddy grunted and nodded.

"Sometimes I just wonder if he should be home more," mama considered.

I couldn't deny the things my parents were saying. It was true, both Garrett and I worked, the only difference was, he had a lot of downtime, and I had very little. But I enjoyed my girls. We did everything together. Five years into the marriage, I'd traveled to Oxford, Ohio to pursue my Bachelor of Science Degree in Education. I had taken my daughter with me. Then, whenever Garrett traveled overseas to play football with his team, I remained at home, taking care of my daughter, spending quality time. I didn't mind my role. In fact, there was nothing I enjoyed more, but hearing my parents' concerns produced a thread of discomfort.

I shook it away.

"It's okay," I assured them. "The Bible says that the man is the head of the household, and a wife is his help mate. I support Garrett to the fullest, and there's no doubt in my mind that he supports me, just the same."

Mama and Daddy smiled and shifted the angle of discussion.

My muscles relaxed.

A few hours later, the girls and I were heading home, and I was surprised to notice that the house was in complete darkness.

My husband was not yet home. I was accustomed to that, but tonight, it felt lonely.

I frowned. "Gracelyn, you're worrying about nothing," I muttered, marching into the baby's bedroom. She was on the brink of sleep, and I changed her out of her clothes and eased her into the crib. I dutifully checked on my other daughter who was settling down, then I headed for the kitchen to make a bottle for the baby, but the ringing phone diverted my attention.

I paused for a second and decided to answer.

My friend Virginia's voice, sounded off. "Gracelyn, hi, do you have a minute?"

My brows drew together. Virginia sounded frazzled, something that was uncharacteristic of her. We'd been friends for years. Our relationship was lighthearted and good-natured; but the tenor of her tone worried me. I had never heard her sound like this. I could tell, something was wrong.

"Hey Virginia, yeah... I mean..." I looked towards the bedroom and uncoiled the long phone cord, pulling it into the kitchen. "To be honest, I don't have a lot of time," I clarified. "I'm about to settle the kids; but what's on your mind?"

Virginia huffed and stalled.

My expression pinched. "Virginia, is everything okay?"

"No, it's not," was her frank reply. "Listen, I don't know how to say this, so I'm just going to come out and let you know what's going on." She paused. "It's about your husband, Garrett."

I froze. In fact, the entire world stopped moving. My jaw cinched and waited for her to continue.

"My husband and I went to a football game today at National Stadium, and Garrett was there."

"Yeah," I confirmed, "he plays professional soccer every Sunday. His team trains during the week, but on Sundays, they have their games." I shrugged. "Was that all?"

"I wish it was," she said, and then she inhaled. "Garrett was there, but he wasn't alone. In fact, he was there with a woman."

Suddenly, my throat grew thick. I swallowed. "Was it one of the other player's wives?" I asked.

"I don't think so."

"What makes you not think so?" I snapped.

"They were kissing."

My grip tightened around the phone and my hand started to shake.

Virginia continued, unaware of my visceral response to what she was saying. "And then they went around the back of the club."

I swallowed again. It did nothing to reduce the layering. "Did they come back to the club afterwards?" I asked, unable to ignore the strong curiosity.

"I'm not sure," she admitted, "but Gracelyn, I think that Garrett is being unfaithful."

It was the bomb I hadn't seen coming yet had been waiting for.

Where the world had stilled, now it spun, as I tried to wrap my mind around what Virginia was saying to me.

It couldn't be true, I told myself.

But Virginia was a good friend. She'd never call me with misinformation or accusations about Garrett if there wasn't a grain of truth to them. She'd attended my wedding. She'd seen me standing at the altar in my sleek, satin dress, and the sparkling tiara. She'd seen the twenty-foot train and the bridesmaids donning pink gowns. Virginia had been one of the hundreds of guests at the ceremony, spectacularly decorated with pink roses and carnations.

She wouldn't lie about something like this.

Still, I needed to see for myself.

"Who is the woman?"

"I'm not sure," she answered, "but it's a white woman."

My eyes fluttered, as I tried to blink stinging emotion away. "Thank you... Virginia," I said. My tone was clipped. "You are a very good friend. I'll look into this." I paused. "Thank you."

WHEN THE FRONT DOOR finally creaked open, it was well after midnight. That was normal. I was accustomed to being asleep by the time my husband arrived home every night. It was normal, but it was different. It was different because this time I knew the truth about what was happening. Never would I have imagined that my husband, the man who supported me and our dreams with his attention and his finances, was a liar and a cheat, but I had been presented with critical information, and by the grace of God, I was going to confront him about what I'd been told.

But not tonight.

Garrett pushed the bedroom door open, allowing dim light from the hallway to seep through the crack, and I squeezed my eyes closed, pretending I was asleep. Slowly, he approached the bed, and when he pressed a kiss on top of my head, hot tears lined the edges of my eyes.

After a while, he changed into his pajamas and eased into the bed next to me, pulling me into, what should have been, a loving embrace.

The next Sunday, after the service had ended, I approached one of the elders.

I needed advice.

Seven days had passed, and I had not confronted Garrett. Each time I attempted to, the world would start to spin, and I'd become paralyzed with debilitating emotions. I could feel myself unraveling. The threads of my sanity were being compromised, but there was no way I could crumble. Not yet. I still needed to know the truth.

I pulled Elder Simons to the side. "I need some Godly advice," I whispered. I scanned the sanctuary, conscious of who might be hearing the conversation, but all of the parishioners were embracing and discussing the goodness of the Lord.

No one was listening to my conversation.

Elder Simons frowned and took my hand into his. "Of course, Sister Gracelyn. Whatever I can do to help, I will. What is on your mind?"

I inhaled. "Last week I learned that my husband is being unfaithful to our vows," I whispered. "There's a... strong possibility that he's committing adultery."

Elder Simons swallowed a gasp. "Are you sure about this, Sister Gracelyn? Your husband, Garrett, is a wonderful man. It's too bad that he doesn't come to church to learn about God's love, but we know that God is working on his heart." He paused and lowered his gaze. "Are you sure about this?"

"Well, that's the thing," I continued. "I haven't talked to him about it as yet. I wanted to speak with the elders and find out what you thought I should do in this situation."

A heavy silence dropped between us.

Elder Simons opened and closed his mouth a few times, before he finally offered his wisdom. "Sister Gracelyn, you must wait on the

Lord," he advised. "The Bible says that when we do this, it is then that He renews our strength."

I nodded, but my neck was stiff.

"God knows everything, and He knows what's best. I will be praying for your strength." With that, he clasped my hands into his, and I figured we were about to pray, but then, he walked away.

Wait on the Lord...

I'd heard that scripture before. In fact, Elder Simons had preached about it a couple of Sundays ago. At the time, I had been certain I knew what it meant, but for some reason, in that moment, it didn't seemed applicable. How was I supposed to *wait* when my husband, the man who had promised to love, honor, and cherish me, was in the streets with another woman?

Elder Simons had offered his advice, but I didn't understand it.

There would only be one thing that would satisfy me. I would need to take matters into my own hands.

Something came over me. Following Garrett and trying to find out what he was up to became an obsession. Many nights, I'd pile the sleeping girls into the car, wrapped up in blankets, and trail Garrett. I stayed a distance behind making sure he never saw me. And whenever the mail came, I'd open it and look for clues of his betrayal. Whenever he slept, I'd stare at him in the darkness, questions and doubt rolling around in my mind like tumbleweed. The anxiety and jealousy ate me from the inside out. My behavior was becoming uncharacteristic, and it didn't seem as if there was anything I could do about it.

Several more days passed.

Garrett was standing in the mirror, brushing his hair. "Sweetheart, I'm going to spend some time with the boys tonight," he announced.

I sat on the bed, body stiff. "Of course, honey," I agreed. I cleared my throat. "Do you think you'll be out for long?"

"I'm not sure," he said with a shrug. He gave his hair a final stroke and then turned to face me. He walked over to the bed and placed an affectionate kiss on my lips. "Don't wait up," he suggested. "Just in case I don't get home early. You have work in the morning, and you need your rest."

I smiled and nodded. I wanted to remind him that he, also, had work in the morning, and the he, also, needed his rest; but I didn't; and as he left the house, I knew that tonight would be the night I would discover the truth for myself.

I waited for an hour. Everything in me wanted to leap off the bed and follow him down the road the minute he'd left the house, but I forced myself to stay put. Then, when enough time had expired, I gathered the girls and piled them into the car.

By now, I'd gathered some information about the woman, I now knew. I'd followed him around enough and I knew the woman's address as if it were my own. I even knew her name. I drove myself and the sleeping girls to the location where I'd been informed that she lived. I had barely parked in the shadows before I spotted him.

Not just him; him and a woman.

A white woman.

And as if the scene that Virginia had described was destined to replay itself, I gawked in disbelief as I witnessed my husband kiss this woman, as if she was his wife and not me.

Tears poured from my eyes. My body shook with disbelief. A moan of pain flew from my lips, but I cupped my hands over my mouth, for fear that I would wake the girls. There was no way I could let them see or hear me like this. It took fifteen minutes for me to compose myself and drive home. When I arrived, I tucked the girls into their beds and buried myself under my own covers.

When Garrett arrived home at some ungodly hour that morning, I pretended I was asleep, even though I was wide awake.

Three days later, I could take no more. By then, sleep was elusive, and I was barely eating. There was no way I could continue living a lie with a man who was living a double life.

He was heading out the door, soccer gear in hand; but before he passed the threshold, I called out to him.

"Garrett."

He paused and turned to face me. The look of love and concern spread across his features was compelling, and I couldn't help but think that he should be nominated for an Emmy.

My jaw stiffened. I tried to think of ways to broach the conversation, ways that were appropriate and gentle. I had been ruminating for weeks, and had devised several strategies, but now, in this moment, I realized there was only one way to address the issue.

"Are you sleeping with another woman?"

Garrett's eyes widened, and his jaw slackened, but he didn't immediately respond.

His vacillation produced waves of rage and disbelief deep inside of me. "I asked you a question," I reminded him.

He rubbed his jaw. "Yes."

I balked. "Are you serious?" I shouted. "Are you really going to just stand there and admit it? Don't you have anything to say for yourself?"

Garrett's shoulders stiffened and he lifted his chin. "There is nothing for me to say," he replied. "You asked me a question and I answered it. I'm seeing another woman and... we've been together for a long time now."

"What do you mean, a long time?"

"That doesn't matter," he snapped.

My mouth clamped shut.

Garrett stared at me but offered no additional information.

"How did you meet her?" I demanded.

Garrett sighed. "Gracelyn, do these details really matter?" he begged of me. "You wanted to know the truth, and now you do. That should be good enough."

"Well it isn't!" I contested.

He groaned and started to head out of the door.

In an instant, I lunged from where I was standing and gripped his arm. "Garrett, if you walk out of this door..." My eyes were burning. "You choose," I spat at him. "It's either her or me. Make your decision now and be prepared to live with it."

Garrett sighed and shook his head. He pressed his eyes closed. "You're backing me into a corner like a rat, Gracelyn!"

"You sound ridiculous," I charged him. "How can I be backing you into a corner, when you're the one who is being unfaithful?" I jerked his arm. "Her or me, Garrett."

"Her!"

I gasped and dropped his arm.

He shrugged. "There, are you happy now? This is all your fault! If you hadn't been so insistent in forcing me to choose between her and you, now – and perhaps later on down the road – things might have been different, but this is where we are now." He scoffed. "I'm going to put an ad in the Royal Gazette," he mocked me. "A good wife and mother; she cleans, cooks, and teaches. Available immediately!"

My jaw dropped as I glared at him in disbelief. My heart was beating faster than a racehorse. Before I could think of a response, Garrett sucked his teeth and marched out of the door. He returned later that night, but the same routine would play out for months: him leaving and me following in the dead of night.

And then a few months later, on Father's Day, I came home to find him leaving with a few of his bags.

I didn't say a word as he walked out of the door.

He had moved out.

It didn't take long for the tapestry of my sanity to unravel, and it was at that point I made the decision to receive professional, psychiatric assistance. For two days, I remained in the psychiatric hospital, engaging in therapy, trying to understand why I hadn't been good enough for my husband. I talked to doctors and processed the issues, but I also talked to God; and it was His response that made the most significant impact in my life:

'Daughter, you chose him. Not me.'

Suddenly, the light came on. I had been attending church and praying, but I had put my husband on a pedestal. I had been serving him, and not God. I had devoted all of my affection to Garrett and failed to acknowledge God in all His ways, the way the Bible had admonished me to do.

I didn't need therapy anymore. God had revealed the root of my problem, and with this knowledge, I would march off into the future, better and wiser.

Or so I thought...

Diary Entry #3 Date: February 18, 1981

I AM AT PEACE

I am at peace
I struggle no more
My heart is not sore
I am at peace
My pain is stripped away
God's love is here to stay
He is the way
I am at peace
My mind, my soul,
My body restored
Exploding joy galore
I am at peace

Chapter Seven
A Drastic Decision

Drastic times call for drastic measures. This was the mantra I recited over and over, even as I made my way to the King Edward Memorial Hospital to embark upon the spontaneous idea that had popped into my mind: a tubal ligation. I had toyed with the thought for weeks, ever since that low-life Garrett had decided to choose his mistress over his wife and his family. I had completed months of therapy and come to terms with the new Gracelyn. I was stronger and I was wiser. Never again would I allow a man to impregnate me and leave me with a newborn baby, while he frolicked and sowed his wild oats. I would take complete control of my body, and this was one of the ways in which I would do so.

I marched through the entrance of the hospital and approached the nursing station. My jaw was set tight as I waited for the nurse to complete whatever task she was doing and attend to me.

"Good morning, ma'am. How may I help you?"

"Good morning," I snapped. I cleared my throat. "I'm here for a tubal ligation procedure."

"Certainly, ma'am. Let me just get your file and I'll have you checked in."

I offered her a tight smile and tapped my nails against the desk, waiting.

A few seconds passed, and after a while, the nurse frowned. "Ma'am, I'm sorry: what is your name?"

"Gracelyn," I answered. "Gracelyn Love."

The nurse's frown deepened. "Mrs. Love, I apologize, but I don't see your name in today's calendar for a scheduled procedure. I don't even see a file with your name on it."

I shifted my weight from one foot to the other.

The nurse peered at me, and her eyes dropped to my ring-finger. "Does... your husband know that you're here?"

My neck snapped back. "I beg your pardon?"

She chuckled and swiped at the back of her neck. "Believe it or not, sometimes we get female patients who come in and request this procedure, without their husbands' permission." She paused. "Where is your husband? Why is he not with you? Did you get his permission, Mrs. Love?"

I glared at the nurse, unable to mitigate my fury. I slammed my palms on the desk and leaned into her face. "I didn't get his permission to be here, just like he didn't get my permission to sleep with another woman and abandon his wife and two daughters!"

The nurse gasped and her hand flew to her chest.

I continued. The words slid between my clenched teeth. "This is my body," I informed her, just in case she didn't know. "I get to decide what I want to do with it!"

The nurse nodded, her head bobbing on top of her neck, eyes wide. "I... understand," she stuttered. "If you just hold on for a few minutes, I'll page the doctor, who will speak with you."

I tugged on the hem of my jacket and took a seat in the waiting area.

Fifteen minutes later, a doctor arrived. He stopped at the nursing station, and I watched as the nurse, no doubt, updated him with the details of my predicament. His mouth dipped into a frown, and after a second, he approached.

"Good morning, Mrs. Love. I'm Doctor Smith. How can I help you today?"

I told him the same thing I'd told the nurse, verbatim, and he folded his arms over his chest. "Mrs. Love, I understand that you're eager to engage in this procedure, but it's not a walk-in service. Protocol requires that you are referred by your general practitioner, and as you know, you haven't been referred so..."

"Doctor Smith," I pleaded with him. By now all of my anger had dissipated. I was emotionally exhausted. I needed for this man to understand the extent of my pain. "I am fully aware of the protocol," I acknowledged. "But you don't understand. I was married. For ten years, I was married to a man who made me believe that he was in love with me. I was a good wife," I said. Unshed tears made my eyes sting. "I did everything I could to be a good wife to that man, to make him happy." I lowered my tone and my jaw cinched. "He left me," I revealed. "After giving him two daughters and everything else I had, he walked away. So you see, this is something I have to do. For the first time ever, I want to do something for myself. I..."

My words disappeared behind a barrage of tears, and the doctor's eyes softened. He reached out and took my hand into his. "Okay, Mrs. Love, there's no need to be emotional," he urged me.

I tried to swallow the tears, but it was no use.

"Mrs. Love, what are the names of your general practitioner and obstetrician?"

"My doctor's name is Jones," I told him quickly. "I spoke with him last week about this. I admit, I don't think he had time to make the arrangements."

"He didn't," the doctor confirmed, "but you may be in luck. Your doctor is actually in the hospital right now. Take a seat while I speak with him. Let's see what we can work out."

The doctor marched away, and I wanted to sit and wait patiently, as he'd suggested, but I was too anxious. Instead, I paced the floors and tried to calm myself by studying the sterile and uninteresting décor of the ward. It seemed to take forever, but soon, my doctor's familiar, yet stern face appeared around the corner.

I rushed in his direction, trying to bridle overwhelming emotion.

"This is very unorthodox," he admitted, speaking to both me and his colleague. "But I gave her a full physical and examination last week, and as such, I feel comfortable to authorize the procedure, especially since this is something she's so adamant about."

I clasped my hands and dropped into the seat behind me, waiting for the arrangements to be put in place. Apparently, they had to find an operating room, and then, a recovery room for after the procedure was complete.

No one would ever know about this, I told myself. Not my parents, not my friends, and especially not my estranged husband, Garrett.

Chapter Eight
Kenneth

Everything I thought had been real, reality had disputed it. I was ready to move on and start a new chapter. I needed to get out of Bermuda and away from the reminders of a love lost – one I probably never really had. Every day that passed saw me become more bitter. I was on the verge of doing something horrible to my soon-to-be ex-husband and his new girlfriend. I needed to get away before that happened.

I sipped on my water, when suddenly, a tall, good-looking man approached my table. A handsome smile creased his mouth, and his eyes seemed to glitter when he looked at me.

"Excuse me, Miss," he started, leaning in a little. "I've been admiring you all night long and couldn't help but notice that frown on your face."

I stiffened in my seat as I took him in: chocolate skin and a confident demeanor. Suddenly, thoughts of my no-good soon-to-be ex-husband were evaporating like a puff of smoke.

The man tilted his head to the empty chair. "Do you mind if I take a seat?" he asked. "I'd sure like to try and turn your frown upside down."

"No, I don't mind at all," I agreed, clearing my throat.

He pulled out the chair and eased into the space. "My name is Kenneth," he introduced himself. He extended his hand and I took it gingerly.

"Gracelyn Love," I replied.

By the time the night ended, Kenneth and I were completely enraptured with one another. I learned that he was a New Yorker, visiting the island on vacation, and I shared with him the things that had recently happened: how my husband had left me for another woman; how I was in the process of divorcing him; how I was still trying to catch myself and come to terms with everything that had gone down.

Kenneth grimaced, horrified by the details of the story. "I just don't get it," he muttered. I don't understand how a man could treat a woman, as beautiful as you are, so poorly." He huffed. "Gracelyn, I'm so sorry this has happened to you," he muttered. The corners of his eyes crinkled with concern.

"Thanks," I said. "It was very painful, but I'll be a better woman for it. True love will come my way, I'm sure of it."

Kenneth smiled. "Maybe you're already looking at it," he commented.

My breath hitched, and when Kenneth grazed the back of his knuckles against my trembling jaw, my face flushed. I tore my stinging eyes away.

"I should get going," I mumbled. I picked up my purse and pushed the chair back.

Kenneth stood next to me. "I understand," he said. "It's getting late and we've been talking for hours." He walked me to the door and didn't hesitate to take my hand into his.

Kenneth continued. "Gracelyn, I'm here for a few more days, but I'd really like to see you again," he requested. "Tomorrow night, meet me back here."

I smiled, unable to resist the puppy-dog look in those brown eyes.

"I'd like to see you again too," I admitted.

We made plans to meet again the next night, and the one after that. On the third night, he was preparing to return to New York. My heart weighed a ton as I watched him pack his things. It had only been three days, but we'd grown close. We'd spent so much time together, touring the island, going out to dinner, and getting to know one another. We'd developed a bond, and to think that it would be over in a matter of hours, tugged at me.

I helped him put a few things into his suitcase and he called me over to him. "Gracelyn, I've had such a wonderful time meeting and getting to know you," he said holding my hand in his. "I really don't want our time together to end."

"I feel the same way," I admitted. "I feel like I'm losing a special part of me."

"I... have an idea," he said.

My eyebrows quirked with curiosity.

"You may think it's crazy," he continued, "but I feel so strongly about you, and I can't imagine not having you in my life." Kenneth paused and drew in a mighty breath. "Gracelyn, let's get married," he blurted out.

I gasped and pulled my hands out of his. I covered my mouth. "You can't be serious," I charged him. "Kenneth, it's only been three days!"

"You're right," he said, "but I'm old enough to know when I've met the woman I want to spend the rest of my life with. You're beautiful, you're intelligent, and you're kind," he listed off. "Gracelyn, you're everything I've ever wanted in a wife. Please, say yes. Let's get married."

I gawked at him, unable to believe the proposal he had put forth, yet something inside of me tingled with excitement. Kenneth was right: we were both grown. I'd just come out of a twelve-year marriage and had learned so much about myself. I knew what I wanted and what I didn't want. I knew what I would tolerate and refused to put up with. I knew the qualities that made a good man, and Kenneth espoused each and every one of them.

Kenneth was my way out of Bermuda. He was the new start I'd been praying for.

A slow smile took my mouth, and I rushed into his open arms, agreeing to his proposal.

KENNETH RETURNED TO the US and immediately began the paperwork process, including obtaining Green Cards for me and the girls. On my end, I worked quickly to resign from my teaching position. I did not care about the house. My house was not a *home*. Love did not live there. Therefore, I left everything in *that house*. My heart was broken and I needed to escape.

Later, the house was sold and the money from the sale was divided. The relief at knowing I was leaving the island was like a weight off my chest. Finally, I was packing up my girls and heading off. My older daughter was headed for Canada, where she was going to spend the summer with her godmother. My youngest daughter and I landed in New York, excited to begin the new journey.

The airplane soaring through the clouds was a visual representation of me: I was like this big, silver bird, flying to new heights. The minute we arrived in New York, Kenneth was waiting for us. The smile on his face rivaled the splendor of the shining, New York sun. We crashed into a warm embrace, and Kenneth swept my daughter up into his arms.

"Gracelyn, you have no idea how happy I am that you agreed to be my wife. I'm excited about our future together."

"So am I," I agreed.

Kenneth whisked us away to what would be our new home. It was a quaint, charming space in an apartment complex. Security roamed the perimeter, and it was clear that it was a safe neighborhood. The door opened and immediately, the aromas of a homecooked meal wafted into the air.

"Don't tell me you cooked!" I said strolling inside. I took in my surroundings. Everything was neat and in order. Yes, this could definitely be my new home, I confirmed. This was just the thing I needed.

Kenneth dragged my suitcases into the house and chuckled. "I wanted to put my best foot forward," he said pulling me into a hug.

"But don't get too excited about it. I'm a provider. I bring home the bacon. It's your job to cook it."

He winked and I smiled. "Well that's a good thing," I commented. "I can make some mean bacon."

We laughed and spent the rest of the day settling into our new home and routine.

The weeks flew by, and before I knew it, Kenneth and I were celebrating four months of being married. By now, summer had ended and my older daughter had come to New York; the challenges that came with a new marriage and relocation were becoming a little more obvious. My older daughter had started school and my younger daughter was in daycare and I was still looking for a job. I had my Bachelor Degree, as well as other teaching credentials, so I assumed it would only be a matter of time before I landed something. Still, I couldn't help but notice that Kenneth seemed to be getting agitated.

Earlier that morning, I had escorted my girls to their individual sites. Now, I was back at home. I turned off the stove and prepared his breakfast plate. Now, my husband was getting ready to go to work. He flipped the newspaper open and took a sip of his coffee, just as I placed the plate in front of him.

"So I applied for another teaching position," I said taking the seat next to him.

"Did you?" he asked, though the paper barely moved from his face.

"Yeah," I confirmed. "I feel pretty good about it. I have all of the experience they require, so I'm definitely a suitable candidate."

Silence.

I moistened my lips. "Do you think I should call and ask about the status of my application?" I pressed him. "I'm just wondering if – "

Kenneth dropped the paper to the table and reached for his briefcase. "Gracelyn, let's talk about this later," he suggested, pushing the chair back. His tone was tight, like it was about to snap. "If I don't leave now, I'll be late, and there's no way that can happen."

I tried to smile, but it felt weak on my face.

Kenneth shrugged into his blazer and headed for the door, but before he passed the threshold, he turned around and pinned his eyes on me. "By the way," he said, "while I'm at work, there are some things I need you to tend to."

I blinked a few times. "Sure, honey. What is it?"

Kenneth rattled off a list of chores that needed to be completed, including the ironing, washing the dishes, making the beds, and cleaning the windows.

My neck jerked back with shock. "You need all of those things done by the time you return?" I asked for clarification.

"Is that going to be a problem?"

A tense silence fell between us.

I cleared my throat and smiled. "No, of course not," I agreed. "I mean, you're going to be working all day and I don't have a job yet. Making sure the house is tidy is the least I can do, right?"

Kenneth smiled and walked out of the door.

I spent the entire day making sure I attended to my husband's request. I'd been married before this, but Kenneth was a new man and I wanted to impress him. He had chosen a good woman, I reminded myself, and he'd know it when he got home. I ironed all of the clothes and folded them into neat piles. Then, I'd filled a bucket with hot, soapy water, and washed the windows, until pure, unfiltered New York sunlight shone through. I'd made the beds right after he left. The final touch was to prepare dinner and have it ready, so that as soon as he came home, I'd be able to give him a good meal.

At around three o'clock, I hurried to pick up my daughters. We chatted about their day as we rushed back to the apartment.

Late afternoon came quickly, and I was just putting the final touches on dinner when Kenneth came through the front door.

"Hey honey, how was work?" I called over my shoulder; but I couldn't help but notice the grimace on his face.

Work must not have gone all that well today...

Kenneth marched over to the folded clothes, which were still sitting on the couch. He snatched up one of his dress shirts and held it in the air. "What's this?" he demanded. His eyes were narrow and menacing.

I wiped my hands on my apron and approached, confused about his question. "That's your white shirt," I reminded him. "The one you wear to work."

Kenneth pinched the bridge of his nose and I frowned, not understanding what I'd missed. "Ken, what's the matter?"

"The matter is that this is not the way clothes are supposed to be folded." The words slid between his clenched teeth and he jerked the shirt until it unfolded in his hands.

"Of course it is," I challenged him, snatching it. "I don't need to remind you, I was married for twelve years, and I folded clothes every weekend." I said this while remodeling the shirt. When I was finished, I rested it back on the pile of clothes. "See? Just like that."

"Your ex-husband might have liked his clothes folded any old way, but that is not my expectation."

Kenneth took me by the arm, and I winced at the way his fingers wrapped around my skin. He dragged me to the bedroom and threw the closet door open.

I gasped at the sight.

All of his shirts were hung meticulously in order of color and season, short-sleeved for summer and long-sleeved for winter. For a minute, he didn't say anything. Instead, he let me watch and draw conclusions about his... expectations.

I blinked away sudden tears.

"This is what I require," he whispered. "Do you have any questions about it?"

"N-no," I muttered.

"Good." Finally, he released my arm, and I fought the urge to rub the now tender spot.

Suddenly, he spun around and glared at the bed. "You didn't make the bed," he snapped.

I was about to open my mouth and object, but I had a feeling that, just like the clothes, things hadn't been done according to his expectations.

Kenneth grabbed a penny from a jar on the dresser and began to drop it on top of the mattress, over and over, until I had no choice but to ask:

"What are you doing?"

"You see this?" he snapped. "If this had been done correctly, this coin would bounce on the bed." The coin dropped with a final thud and he turned to face me.

"Kenneth, you can't be serious," I said chuckling, trying to lighten the mood, but his eyes narrowed and his mouth thinned into a straight line.

"This is no laughing matter," he seethed. "When I give you chores to complete, I expect them to be done properly."

My breath hitched, and my eyes flitted to the girls' bedroom. Thank God they were in there with the door closed, watching television. The last thing I wanted was for them to hear the rantings of this crazy man.

He continued, "After the girls are gone to bed, I'll oversee your routine, just to make sure you're doing everything according to – "

"Your expectations..." I filled in.

He grunted and marched out of the room.

Chapter Nine
Shackled

Time progressed, but each day saw my new husband displaying new, authoritative behaviors. By now I'd learned to make the bed according to his specifications; and his clothes were now hung according to color and sleeve length. I wanted to be a dependable wife. I'd envisioned such a wonderful life with my new husband, and I was trying my best to meet his needs, as well as those of my daughters; however, it always seemed as if my efforts weren't good enough.

And it started to wear me down.

I took the girls to school and Kenneth was at the table waiting for his breakfast before he headed to work. I was still job hunting, but I had also learned that Kenneth wasn't open to hearing the details of my search. I didn't understand it, but the topic of me working seemed to anger him. Anytime I brought the topic up, he'd offer a snarky comment or ignore me all together. Because of that, I started keeping these details to myself. I couldn't wait to secure a job. All I did was stay at home and make sure the house was tidy, while Kenneth and the girls were out.

I put my husband's breakfast plate together, making sure everything was prepared just the way he liked. "Here you go," I said easing the steaming plate down in front of him. "You go ahead and eat while I finish cleaning the kitchen," I suggested, heading for the sink. I dipped my hands into the water and was washing the cutlery, when suddenly, Kenneth's stark tone interrupted.

"What are you doing?" he barked.

I froze, hands still submerged in the water.

What in the world was he on about now? When I looked at him, his shoulders were rigid, and his eyes looked as if torches had been lit in them.

"Kenneth…" I pushed out a breath, trying to coax myself into patience. "What's the matter?"

"You're asking me what the matter is?" He jabbed his finger in my direction. "Is that the proper way to place silverware in the drainer?" His voice was low. "How many times do I have to tell you? Show you?" He stomped to where I was standing and ripped the fork from my shaking hands. I startled when he slammed it into the drainer, right-side up.

Kenneth stood back, breathing over me like an enraged bull. "When are you going to learn?" he whispered. "When are you going to start doing things properly around here?"

I cowered under his gaze with his shoulders folded forward. Why couldn't he see that I had been trying? From the moment I'd agreed to marry him, I'd been trying to obtain his gold star of approval, but nothing I did was good enough. I was becoming tired of the criticism and judgement. It had gone on for so long, I felt more like his servant, as opposed to his wife, the one he'd promised to love, cherish, and protect.

My jaw trembled, but I unlocked it. "Do I look like a maid?" I questioned him boldly. "Do I have the word 'maid' written on my forehead?"

Kenneth didn't reply right away, but his eyes stretched wide and his nostrils flared. "You would dare talk back to me?" he demanded in a seething whisper. "You think you're a maid, do you? Let me show you how maids get treated by me."

Kenneth spun on his heel and marched for the bedroom. Instantly, apprehension threaded itself around my throat and I rushed after him.

"Kenneth, wait," I called out. I reached out to grab his arm, but he jerked away.

"So, you think I treat you like a maid? Okay..." he was grumbling to himself, stomping through the house like a soldier on a mission.

I stumbled after him, offering words of useless apology.

When he reached our bedroom, he threw the door open and headed for the bed. I watched, in dismay, as he started to dismantle it, piece by piece.

"Kenneth, what are you – "

"What does it look like I'm doing?" he barked before I could even finish asking the question. "I don't sleep with maids, which means I won't be sleeping with you!"

Tears sprang from my eyes and I begged him to reconsider. I'd spoken out of turn, I said, and now, I could see his point about the cutlery. I was grateful for everything he was doing for me and the girls. I tried to tell him, but he didn't listen. By the time he'd finished his task, my face was wet with hot tears, and I was sobbing uncontrollably.

But Kenneth wasn't finished.

With tears streaking my face, Kenneth began to shove me out of the room. The door slammed closed and I banged my fists against it. "Kenneth, open up!" I called out.

He didn't answer.

I banged again, my fist pulsing in pain. "Don't lock me out," I pleaded.

Still, no answer.

My shoulders slumped as I retreated to my daughters' bedroom, which would become my new room.

TIME DREW ON AND MY husband's refusal to acknowledge me emotionally or otherwise increased. He was always kind to the girls and frequently took them on trips to visit his family, but I was made to stay at home, living out of unpacked boxes and calling my friends and family collect from public telephone booths.

"*Gracelyn, it's so good to hear from you,*" *my parents would say.* "*How is everything? How are Kenneth and the girls?*"

"*Everything is perfect!*" *I'd reply, deliberately adding a healthy dose of cheer into my tone.* "*Things couldn't be better! The girls are wonderful, and Kenneth... well, you know him.*"

And that was the thing: they *didn't* know Kenneth. In fact, nobody did. On the surface, he was pleasant and gentle. Everyone loved him. To them, he was the perfect gentleman. It seemed as if only I knew the truth about who he was.

"*I'm so glad to hear that,*" *Daddy would say.*

Mama would chime in. "*And let us know when we can come and visit, Gracelyn.*"

Oh, how I wished they could. It was yet another thing they didn't know, I wasn't allowed to have visitors.

I'd choke out a response, bid them farewell, and hang up. My secret to bear.

TIME CONTINUED TO PASS, but nothing changed. In fact, my husband's erratic behavior reached new heights. It got so bad, that on one occasion, when the girls had gone to Bermuda to visit their father, I'd waited for Kenneth to leave the house and jumped into a taxi.

"Where you headed?" the driver asked, peering at me through the rear mirror.

I peeked into my purse, just to make sure my passport and credit cards were in it, the way they normally were. "JFK."

I arrived in Bermuda to an empty homestead.

Everyone was at work. I trudged to my bedroom and fell across the bed, into a sound sleep. When my parents arrived home that evening, they were elated and surprised to see me. when they asked what had brought me there and about Kenneth, I supplied a lame excuse. And there I stayed, for seven days. I never left the house and I didn't even tell my girls that I was on the island.

I had many friends, so many of whom had been a positive effect over the course of my life. There was my best friend from elementary school and the girls from college. There was my grandmother, the woman who was my rock! There were times I felt like a fraud for not telling them about the things I was going through. But, how could I? The fear of being judged because of my situation; the shame and the shackles – it was holding me hostage, covering me like a dark, moonless night. There was no way I could tell anyone the things that were happening. I decided that it was best I keep it all to myself.

"HAVE A GOOD DAY, HONEY!" I called out one day, but the door had slammed closed before I'd finished saying it. I sighed and tried to refit my resolve. The girls were in Bermuda with their father and wouldn't be returning for the next two weeks. It was lonely at times without them. They were my roommates, after all. When they were there, they were a welcome distraction. Since the incident, I hadn't been allowed back into the bedroom and now that they were gone, I was left with my thoughts and the reality that my marriage was nothing like I thought it would be. Not only that, Kenneth was nowhere near the man he'd portrayed in the beginning.

I decided to clean around the house and run a few errands before he came home. It wouldn't take me long to get the house in order, especially because cleaning was something I did every day, just to avoid arguments and stay in Kenneth's good book. Soon, I was readying myself to head out. I swung my purse over my shoulder and pushed against the door, but when it didn't shift open, I stood back, shocked. I pushed against it again, and when the same thing happened, I wracked my brain, trying to figure out what the issue could be.

I fiddled with the knob and the lock, but nothing happened. Suddenly, panic started to set in. We only had one door, I thought. If I couldn't get out, what in the world was I going to do? And how in the world could this have happened?

Then it dawned on me...

"Kenneth," I breathed in a whisper of disbelief. "He's done this! He's locked me in, trying to keep me as his prisoner!"

Quickly, I grabbed a piece of paper and a pen. My hand shook as I scribbled words down:

HELP! I'M LOCKED IN APARTMENT #519!

I folded the paper and dashed to the kitchen, where I found a plastic container. Once the note had been secured, I tossed it out of the bathroom window and watched it plummet to the ground below; then I waited for someone to find it and come to rescue me.

It seemed to take forever for someone to respond. After hours of being on edge, one of the security guards who watched the apartment complex was banging on the door. From where I stood inside, I could hear him jerk it a few times, but nothing happened.

I rushed to the door. "Oh my goodness, thank you so much for helping me!" I could barely get the words out. I pressed my hands and face against the door, trying somehow to get closer to the person on the other side of it.

"Ma'am, what seems to be the problem?" the voice called out.

"I'm locked in," I said, harried. "My husband, I don't know how he did it, but I'm trapped inside and I can't get out. Please, do something."

"Okay, ma'am, if you could just calm down..."

"Calm down?" I huffed. "Do you know how long it is that I've been in here? You have to do something!"

"Okay ma'am, let me see what I can do." Suddenly, the door began to rattle as the man tugged on it. To my horror, nothing happened.

How in the world had Kenneth done it? He was trying to cage me, there was no doubt in my mind.

I heard the man sigh behind the barrier. "Ma'am, I'm sorry, but there doesn't seem to be any way to unlatch the door."

"Oh Lord..." I muttered. More tears leaked onto my face.

"But don't worry," he tried to assure me again. "When your husband comes home, I'll speak with him and get him to unlock the door. We'll find out what's going on and get to the bottom of this."

Horror seized me. him telling my husband was the last thing I wanted. If Kenneth found out that I'd been trying to get out or even asked someone for help, there was no telling what would happen. But there was no way I could tell this man that. That would make everything one hundred times worse.

I tried to steady my trembling lip and suck back the tears in my throat. "O-okay," I stuttered. "Thank you."

The hours drew on and each one that passed saw me more anxious. Dark thoughts flitted through my mind, but I tried to swat them away. Soon, the doorknob was twisting and the security officer who had tried to assist me earlier was standing at the door.

But he wasn't alone.

Kenneth stood by his side. A smile was pasted onto his face, but there was no way I'd miss the dark, sinister glare behind his pupils.

"Sir, thank you so much for helping," the security officer said, oblivious to the underlying menace. "As I mentioned to you downstairs, your wife was very frazzled this morning. I found a note she'd thrown out the window." To my dismay, he unfolded the now crumpled paper and handed it to my husband.

Kenneth received it and frowned. "Oh no, sweetheart," he cooed. "Why didn't you call me? I had no idea you were locked inside or upset." His eyes swung up. "Come here, sweetheart." He extended his arms, offering faux sympathy. I meandered closer to him, even though in his embrace was the last place I wanted to be – yet, I was fearful of the alternative.

Kenneth squeezed me and the security officer smiled.

"You see now, Mrs. Gracelyn?" he said. "I told you: once your husband returned everything would be all right."

No, it was all wrong.

"Officer, thank you so much for assisting us. I'll take it from here," Kenneth said.

The man saluted and backed out of the door. The minute it was sealed, the dark glare that had been behind Kenneth's pupils rose full to the surface. He gripped my arm and ripped me into him. "Don't you ever call security on me again," he snarled. His lips barely moved. He jerked me one more time. "And if I ever catch wind that you're trying to leave the apartment and not tend to your chores, you'll be sorry."

I pulled away from him and dashed to the girls' room – my room – and bawled, cursing my existence until the next day.

I ONLY EMERGED FROM my room when I heard the door slam closed the next morning.

Kenneth, the actor, had gone to work.

I had mulled over the events of the past twenty-four hours the entire night. Flashes of victimization and abuse sailed through my mind until I could barely take anymore. There was no way I could continue to exist under these abusive conditions.

I had to do something, I thought.

I had to LEAVE!

The amount of times I'd thanked God that the girls were in Bermuda with their father were too many to count. It meant that I could make the move I needed to make without the extra worry. I could pack up my things and be gone. I could flee and go to a place where Kenneth would never find me. After the crying had stopped, I'd planned it carefully. Now, it was time to put the plan into motion.

I eased the door open. Part of me was afraid that he hadn't really left. He was such an actor. The performance he'd put on in front of that security officer could have won him an award. It was just like the time my best girlfriend from Bermuda had visited me in New York and requested to come to the apartment. I'd begged her not to; not because I didn't want to see her, but because Kenneth didn't allow anyone to visit.

Not even my parents.

Unfortunately, she'd insisted. When she arrived, Kenneth was the perfect gentleman. He was pleasant and cordial and agreed to allow the girls and me to go with my friends. We were going to Junior's Restaurant and Bakery in Brooklyn, to get a slice of their famous cheesecake. I tried to tell her the truth: that Kenneth was pretending. I insisted that when we returned and the girls went to bed, he would lash out at me; but we went anyway and had a wonderful time.

The minute my friends left he jabbed his finger in my face. "Don't you ever let anyone come to this house again. Do you understand?" he snarled.

I'd stormed back into the room I shared with the girls and sealed the door. I gazed at them, stinging tears filling my eyes. "Babies, we will be safe and at peace soon. I promise," I'd whispered.

Now it was time to put that whispered promise into action.

My eyes scanned the area, and when I was certain that I was alone, I rushed to the closet and pulled out a small travel bag. Quickly, I pitched random items inside of it, not caring if they matched or didn't. I only had one focus: reclaiming my life.

Once everything was packed, I rushed for the door. I turned the handle and breathed a prayer of gratitude that it actually opened today, unlike yesterday. I hurtled down the steps, out of the apartment and onto the sidewalk. I hailed the first taxi that I saw and hopped inside.

"Where to, lady?"

"Edison Hotel."

"You got it!"

The taxi whizzed down the street and the further away he drove, the more tension seeped from my pores. When I finally got into my hotel room, I dropped my bags and began to work on the next phase of the plan I'd devised. In the beginning, Kenneth had never wanted to talk about my search for a job, and by the end, it was clear that he didn't want me to have one. Despite his controlling ways, I never deterred from applying for positions. In fact, a former teacher and dear friend had told me about a Head Teacher position at a school in Chinatown. I'd gotten out of the house and I never intended on going back, but now, I'd need a job for sure.

I pulled a piece of paper out of my purse and considered the number written down, for less than a second, before calling and expressing interest in the position. The lady with whom I spoke invited me to come in for an interview.

The following day, I was up bright and early, and I wasted no time heading for Head Start Center, in Chinatown.

The secretary pulled her eyes up from whatever was on her desk as I entered.

"Good morning," I greeted her. I tried to keep my tone chipper, despite the anxiety swirling in my chest. "I'm here to meet the director. She invited me to interview for a position."

"O-of course," the secretary responded, and she pasted a smile onto her face. "I think she's expecting you. Let me show you in."

She led me to the director's office door, and when I pushed it open, the woman stared at me in shock. "Are you... Miss Gracelyn?" she asked.

I narrowed my eyes. "Yes, I am," I responded. "Were you expecting someone else at this time?"

Quite clearly, she hadn't expected a black woman to show up in her office that day. I could tell from the way she tried to relax her expression and soften her tone. "No, not at all," she answered and cleared her throat. "I do apologize, Miss Gracelyn. Please have a seat."

With the interview complete, I returned to my hotel room, where I stayed for the remainder of the day, plotting and planning. The next day, the director of Head Start called to say that I'd gotten the job. I slumped in the desk chair, both relieved and anxious. It had been a long time since I'd worked. From the moment I'd arrived in New York, I'd searched for employment, but Kenneth would always find a way to put a stop to it. But not this time, I won't allow him.

I remained in the hotel for one month and continued to operationalize my plan. I obtained a New York City driver's license and called my father. I asked him to transfer the money I'd received from selling the matrimonial home into my New York bank account, and I started house hunting.

Chapter Ten
Nursed By An Angel?

E ven though I'd returned to the apartment, my plan was in full swing. I had a fulltime job in Chinatown, as Head Teacher, doing what I loved. But Kenneth was still mean and overbearing. I had to find a way to leave him for good. But how? That was the question! Each day I thought of ways of escaping, and it wasn't long before depression found me.

One evening, after the girls had been tucked into their beds, I dropped onto the couch, staring blindly in the distance. Things weren't getting better, and this was never the way I imagined my life would go. I was so young, yet I had been through so much: lies, betrayal, heartache. I was strong. I'd survived and come this far, but there were days when I couldn't imagine going on anymore. There were times when I felt I had no strength left. There were hours when I couldn't imagine existing another minute.

I choked back tears and lifted myself from the couch. My feet started to move of their own accord. They led me to the bathroom, and my fingers wrapped around the medicine cabinet handle. I pulled it open and fished out a bottle of sleeping pills; then, I allowed my feet to lead me further. To the garage.

I sank to the cold, concrete ground, my legs folding under me. I twisted off the bottle's cap and tipped the pills into my mouth. One by one, they slid down my throat, bitter, acidic. I swallowed them back, trying to ignore the thickness lining my throat; and then I sat there waiting for something to happen.

I had no knowledge of how much time had passed. All sound faded into oblivion, but I gathered myself to my feet and ambled for the garage door. My feet continued to lead the way. I wandered a block and a half down the street and around the corner, until I reached the hospital, and when I pushed open the side door, I was greeted by a nurse.

Her face was blurry, but the grimace making her lips turn down could not be missed.

Quickly, she hurried me to a small room. "Ma'am, I need you to vomit," she urged me. Her voice was both calm and authoritative. "Ma'am!" she called again.

My back lurched and I spewed into the porcelain bowl.

"Good," she encouraged me, rubbing my back.

I regurgitated over and over, until nothing but bile was produced.

The nurse rubbed my back. "We need to get you registered," she urged, taking me by the arm.

Everything was a blur, but I was lucid enough to consider the consequences that might come with me doing as she was suggesting. "No," I denied her. "I can't."

"What do you mean? We need to get you checked out," she insisted. "This is a serious matter."

"I can't check in," I repeated. "I won't. I'm a school teacher and if anyone ever found out about this, it could be damaging to my career." I heaved again and my eyes watered. "Also, I have two beautiful daughters," I informed her further. "If I register at the desk, they may call child protective services, and there is no way I'm going to lose my girls to that evil man!"

The nurse sighed, eased me back against a cot, and pulled a blanket up under my chin.

Early the next morning, I got up and went home, before the girls could awaken and find me not there.

DAYS PASSED, AND IT was during that time I realized how low I'd allowed my circumstances to push me. I had to stay strong, I thought to myself. I knew that God had a plan for my life, and there was no way I could allow the lies of the enemy to penetrate me. I thought of the kind nurse, who'd been there for me and assisted me through the dark incident. I needed to see her again and tell her thank you.

A few days later, I walked the same path to the hospital, but when I arrived, she wasn't there. I scanned the area, thinking that maybe she was assisting another patient. When I saw the Head Nurse at the registration station, I approached.

"Good afternoon," I said, smiling warmly at her. "I'm looking for a nurse. I don't know her name, but she was here on Thursday evening, at around ten o'clock, and she was a great help to me. I want to tell her thank you."

The Head Nurse frowned and shook her head. "I'm sorry, what time did you say you were here?"

I didn't want to provide her with details, but it was obvious that I needed to explain a little more. "The nurse who was on the nightshift," I continued. "I wanted to thank her for being so kind and understanding. I met her by that side door," I said, pointing in the direction I'd come in.

"Ma'am, I'm sorry, that's not possible," she finally said. "That door is locked every Thursday night, due to a shortage of staff. There's no way a nurse would have met you there, let alone you gaining entry."

I paused. "The nurse... she was tall, with dark skin, and short curly hair," I began to explain.

The Head Nurse shrugged. "I'm sorry ma'am, no one by that description works on this floor. Are you... sure you came to this hospital? There are other clinics located in the vicinity. Maybe you went to one of those on Thursday night."

I gasped. *The woman who helped me; was she an angel?*

"Okay, I understand," I said, and then I smiled again. "Well thank you – and have a great day."

We waved our goodbyes, and I left the hospital utterly bewildered, yet certain that God had been with me that day. I was right. He had a plan for my life, and there was no way I would let the enemy have the victory.

DIARY ENTRY #4 DATE: February 1983

> **Psalm 34:7:** The angel of the Lord encamped round about them that fear him; and deliver them.

Chapter Eleven
Shut Up Lady

THE NEW YORK BOARD of Education was offering the New York City Teachers' License. I had applied and was accepted to take the exam. Kenneth didn't know this. I'd made the decision not to tell him because I was fearful that if he knew that, he'd deny me from taking it.

Early that morning, I walked to the subway and headed to Columbia University, where the examination was being held. I had walked this route many times to go to the Lexington Subway. The roads were relatively quiet, except for the sounds and sights of early commuters exercising or making their way to work. I hurried along, thinking about my exam, hoping I had studied well and about the goodness of the Lord and all the things He'd done for me up until that point, when suddenly, a hand gripped my arm and dragged me off the sidewalk. Instantly, a piercing shriek lifted in my throat, but the person – whoever it was – they clapped their hand over my mouth. "Shut up, lady!"

I gripped onto a nearby fence, ignoring the piercing pinch of the wire perforating my delicate fingertips. The mugger ripped me off, dragged me several feet, and shoved me into an elevator. I watched in horror as his finger slammed against the button for the top floor. I glared at him: a tall, black man, probably no more than twenty-five years old. Shock had my body quivering, but the more I stared at him, the angrier I became.

"You... you should be ashamed of yourself!" I spat at him. "How dare you rob a black woman? Does your mother know you're doing this? Robbing people?"

His eyes burned with rage. "Shut up, lady!" he yelled.

My jaw cinched. "If you're going to rob somebody, you should go down to Park Avenue, I suggested, tone dripping with sarcasm. "That's where the rich people are!"

"Shut. Up. Lady!" Without offering additional commentary, he began to grope at my arm, removing my expensive, sterling silver bracelets – the ones my father had given me. The ones' whose sentimental value could not be understated.

I jerked my arm out to him. "Yeah, take them," I goaded him, "but you won't get much money for them. They're cheap!"

He frowned and thrust my arm away, disgusted. Still, he didn't relent. He scraped his hand across my throat and ripped my gold necklace away. He also grabbed my purse and removed a fifty-dollar bill.

"That money was to buy my children's food!" I shouted at him.

"Shut up, lady!" he shouted in response.

Finally, the elevator doors hissed open, and the thug hopped off, but not before pressing the ground floor button and sending me shuttling back down. When I finally reached the ground floor, I was completely dazed and disconcerted. The reality of what had happened slapped me in the face like a wet rag.

A woman, who was standing nearby, noticed my befuddled state and instantly called the police. I was shaking like a leaf, and that was when I noticed the scrapes and bruises on my skin, as well as the fact that one shoe had been left on the sidewalk during the ordeal.

"Oh my goodness, I can't believe that just happened to you," the lady said in a harrowed breath. Just then, her husband came rushing from inside the building.

"Don't worry," he assured me. "We're going to stay right here with you until the police officers get here."

The minute the police arrived, the husband, wife, and I explained the things which had occurred.

"Ma'am, we need you to come with us. We're going to take you to the hospital, and then to the police station," the officer informed me, but I shook my head.

"No," I objected emphatically. "I need to take the NYC Teachers' License exam. I was on my way to Columbia University, and that's where I'd like to go, please."

"Are you sure?" the wife asked. "You don't want to press charges?"

"I need to get to the exam," I reiterated. "It's only offered yearly, and there's no way I can miss it. I'll go to the police station later, but right now I really need to go to the university."

I completed my exam, and soon the police were escorting me back to the station. I entered a private room, that looked like the ones in the tv shows. There was a solitary desk and a metal chair. The minute I dropped into it the officer presented me with a huge photograph album. The mugger's face was engraved in my mind. I knew exactly what he looked like.

"Are you ready to identify your attacker," asked the officer

I replied readily, "Yes, I will never forget that face." I started flipping through the album. That was when I saw him. His dark, beady eyes and close, cropped hair jumped off the page at me.

"This is him," I proclaimed, heart racing.

"Are you sure?"

I frowned, as doubt crept in. "You're right," I considered, "I'd better make sure. The last thing I'd want is for the wrong person to be convicted." I turned the pages some more, and suddenly, I was confused. Each time the officer asked if I was certain, I'd say no. I was there for hours, and in the end, I was unsuccessful. The only thing I could remember in certainty, was that the thug had continued to say: "Shut up, lady!"; but there was no way that piece of information would assist in his arrest.

The officer scratched his jaw. "We're not aware of any criminal with that M.O."

"What in the world is a M.O.?"

"Modus Operandi," he answered, and then he sighed. "Well, at least you made it out alive," he said. "You sustained a few minor injuries, but the reality is, you could have died tonight."

And that was when reality set in.

Thank God!

No one in my family, friends, or Kenneth ever knew about the mugging. That was my secret to keep.

Diary Entry #5 Date: March 23, 1983

> **Psalm 140:4:** *Keep me safe, Lord, from the hands of the wicked;*
>
> *protect me from the violent, who devise ways to trip my feet.*

SECRETLY LOOKING FOR a place for my girls and me, without Kenneth's knowledge was arduous. Finally, I secured a wonderful condo in Parkchester, Bronx. It was a community with twenty-four-hour security, beautiful trees, flowers, and playgrounds and a shopping center. I used the money my father had transferred into my account from the sales of the house to get it. Now, I needed a plan to escape from Kenneth's apartment without his knowledge. He always stayed away weekends. Perhaps that would be a good time to escape.

I called several moving companies and I repeated the same story over and over.

"Good morning sir, I need a moving company that can *guarantee* me out of the apartment in record time."

"What do you call record time ma'am?"

"Under forty-five minutes!"

Silence would drop over the line. "That's a short window ma'am," the employee would inform me, as if I didn't already know that, "especially if you have a lot of items to be moved."

I'd try to steady my racing breath. "I don't have many items, just my clothes and my daughters' television. I must be out before my husband comes home," I explained. "If he catches wind of what I'm doing, he'll prevent me from leaving. I know he will." I paused, thinking of something else. "I also have a feeling he'll hurt me this time."

Another moment of silence descended, but this time, I could feel the employee's empathy wafting over the telephone line. "Ma'am, we'll be there," he guaranteed. "If this is a matter of safety, we'll have you out of there in forty-five minutes or less – guaranteed."

On Saturday morning, at six o'clock, they arrived. We took only what was ours, no more, no less. My daughters and I climbed into the moving truck and headed for the Bronx

We had escaped!

FREE AT LAST!

2 Corinthians 4:8,9

We are hard pressed on every side, but not crushed. Perplexed, but not in despair:

Persecuted, but not abandoned, struck down, but not destroyed.

Two years passed before the divorce was final, and to my delight, I never saw or heard from Kenneth or any of his family until my phone rang with the message that he had passed away. I attended his funeral, and as I trailed the line of mourners who were standing at the casket to pay their last respects, I tensed. It would be my first time seeing him since I left the apartment on a whim. When I looked at him a strange sense of relief washed over me. I observed his features and the way the mortician had designed a pleasant smile over his lips, yet the only things I could remember were the frowns and scowls.

"You can't be mean to me anymore, Kenneth," I whispered. Then, I walked away and gave the family my condolences.

Diary Entry #6 Date: September 12,1985

Optimism

Optimism

Positive thinking prevails

Through strife and wails

Optimism endures

Future goals are bright

We step into God's light

Confidence, Positivity

Straight ahead to Victory

James 1:12: Blessed is the man who keeps on going when times are hard. After he has come through, he will receive a crown.

Chapter Twelve
Unavailable Men

I spent the next years of my life beefing up my education, obtaining degrees, including a Master of Education in Early Childhood, Reading Recovery Certifications, Literacy Coach, and Librarian trainings. While it wasn't easy – juggling single parenthood, working, and education – I knew that it was necessary. There were times I'd take my youngest daughter to class with me.

By the time I'd accomplished my academic and professional goals, I was ready to enter the dating scene again. It took me a long time to forgive Garrett and Kenneth for the negative impact they'd had on me, but by the grace of God, I had become stronger and wiser. Now that I was entertaining the idea of relationships again, I knew the signs of a no-good man, and there was no way I'd entertain them.

A few men fell onto my radar over the years, including a businessman and a police officer, but the former resulted in a supportive and loving Godly friendship, while the latter fizzed out, due to work commitments and scheduling. Besides, I often found myself fearing for his life whenever he was out in the streets, and this apprehensive disposition wasn't sustainable, not just for me, but for the relationship in general.

Then there was Rafael, the handsome and exotic Latino. He was suave and debonair, and he added spice and variety to my otherwise routine existence. His accent, thick like honey, would make me feel warm and giggly inside, especially when he would tell me how beautiful and charming I was. And Rafael would cook the most delectable meals, using an array of spices and produce. Whenever we went out dancing, my hips would sway back and forth, of their own accord, to the thumping Latin beats. Whenever he and I were together, I felt as if I could take on the world. But alas, it wasn't meant to be, and like most good things, they come to an end.

I was also open to dating whenever I returned to Bermuda on vacation. By this time, the trips were bittersweet. My parents were deceased, and my only sister and I were estranged. Bermuda was chock full of both good and bad memories; but when I met one man in particular, he seemed to erase the bad completely. Despite the fact that he was very unavailable, we became very good friends. He treated me very kindly and affectionately and made sure that I was happy. There were many sacrifices made, but we were determined to be together because life was short and we gravitated towards love.

It wasn't long before we realized that God wasn't pleased. There were times when we'd pray and read God's word together, but in reflection, both of us realized that we were looking to God to agree with our decisions, even though they were outside of His will. Of course, God never did. Three years after our friendship began, this special man passed away. Sadness gripped me, but I had no choice but to trust God's judgement.

Diary Entry #7 Date: February 19, 2013

The Search is Behind

I searched and searched

Year after year

Dating men who seemed to care

Only to meet men

Who wanted a one night stand

Not for me, needed to end

I prayed and prayed

To God above

But did not heed His word of love

I saw this man who made me laugh

We dated long and had a blast

I thought this man is mine

At last, my search is past.

> *Exodus 20:3: You shall have no other gods before me.*

> **Matthew 22:37: And he said to him, "You shall have loved the Lord your God with all your heart and with all your soul and with all your mind."**

Chapter Thirteen
Leopold

Five Years Later

"Three's a charm!" That's what I was saying to myself the moment I met Leopold while on a blind date with a good friend. Goodness, I'd seen some handsome men before, but Leopold had to have taken the cake! He wasn't tall in stature, but he carried himself as if he was. He was dark, and impeccably handsome, and the minute our eyes locked, it was love at first sight. Certainly, this was the man I had been destined to grow old with. After everything I'd been through, God had preserved Leopold just for me.

And I deserved it. I deserved to be happy. I'd endured years of verbal and mental abuse. I'd been belittled and shackled, both literally and emotionally. I'd experienced unfaithfulness and betrayal. I radiated happiness and contentment to the world, but inwardly, pain ground and gnashed my heart.

But now, with Leopold...

There was nothing Leopold wouldn't do for me. He was a master chef, who could whip up scrumptious dishes in a heartbeat. Not only that, Leopold cleaned up after himself, unlike Kenneth who thought I was his personal slave. He was also meticulous about the way he dressed. Leopold would spend hours in the bathroom, making sure that his attire was on point. It was an admirable quality. He was well-groomed and took pride in his appearance, just like I did. The fulfillment of Leopold's love erupted like fireworks, originating from deep inside of me. Finally, I was content; completely satisfied.

And then everything changed.

Leopold's grooming habits were always very precise, but soon I began to notice that there was more attention to detail on the weekends. His wardrobe became more fashionable and trendy.

And he was coming home later and later.

Sometimes, not coming at home at all, until the next day.

Something wasn't right.

When January 1, 2000 arrived, it was the beginning of a new season for me. Leopold had gone out celebrating, the way he always did, but I sat on the bed alone vowing to myself anew that there was no way in heaven or earth that I would go through this again. I'd been there and done that – gotten the postcard. If Leopold thought I was going to sit back like a good wife, while he was having an affair, he had another thing coming.

But how would I approach him? This had been going on for quite some time now, and in the past I'd come right out and demanded answers; but Leopold would always respond with a calm and collected tone, telling me that it was all in my mind, and that there was no way he'd ever cheat on me.

"Sweetheart, you're everything I need," he affirmed me. "You're a wonderful woman and a wonderful wife. Why would you ever think I'd want someone other than you?" After uttering these words of affection, he'd press a tender kiss on my mouth.

He was right, I thought. He was perfect in every way. He was loving, caring, and attentive – a stark difference from my two ex-husbands.

Still... something wasn't sitting right. It was a feeling sitting in my gut, like a lump of coal. I wanted to believe Leopold, but somehow, there was this nagging doubt that wouldn't leave me alone. I needed to accrue evidence, I thought. I needed a clear and concise plan. I'd seen

Judge Judy on Court TV and remembered the way she required evidence for her judgements.

Whenever Leopold's credit card statements arrived in the mail, he would open them and leave them on the dresser. When he wasn't at home, I'd follow behind and make copies of them. He also had a cell phone, and I did the same thing whenever his cell phone bill arrived. Each month I collected evidence. Not only that, I searched for patterns – toll payments, restaurant charges, recurring telephone numbers, clothing purchases – anything that struck me as being a *red flag*. I kept a meticulous log of his comings and goings and made a folder dedicated to all of the data I'd collected.

Years marched on, and Leopold continued to come and go as he liked. Every now and then, I'd raise the issue, but my concerns were ignored. Our discussions would turn into arguments and life was slowly but surely transforming. Where it had once been bliss, now it was unbearable. My marriage had sunk to the depths of a bottomless pit. At home, he was the perfect man, but that was never the problem. The issue was that he was rarely *at* home!

At work, I kept up the jovial façade. Secrets, shame and shackles smothered me like a raging wildfire; but my main objective was to ensure my daughters' wellbeing and safety. I had to push on. I had to stay strong. I needed to depend on God to bring me through, the way He had in the past. He had never let me down. He had never left or forsaken me, just like He'd promised in his Word.

But it was hard.

One night, while the girls were asleep, Leopold left to go and socialize, the way he always did – and I followed him. His car zoomed along the highways and byways, and into Southern Boulevard, in the Bronx. I trailed behind and watched as he parked his car outside of a bar and went in.

Slowly, I exited my vehicle and eased into the dimly-lit, crowded bar, making sure he was not aware of my presence. I remained in the shadows. Watching. Leopold clinked a glass of red wine against a friend's glass and threw his head back in laughter. A few women threw their arms around his neck and pulled him onto the dancefloor. He was having a great time, while I was at home waiting and...

I stumbled out of the exit, disturbed and distressed. I threw my car door open and peeled away from the curb, rage blinding me. How dare he leave me at home and go out, enjoying himself? The thought was like a shriek in my brain. I sealed my eyes and stepped on the gas. The car gunned through the streets and the blare of passing vehicles split my eardrums.

I didn't care.

I didn't want to live. I was tired of the merry-go-round, the cycle. I was a good woman, full of life, and love. Why did I continue to find myself involved with men who just didn't care?

By now, the pedal was to the metal. More horns screamed and the car rattled on the street. The sound of the gears shifting seeped into my mind, but suddenly, I opened my eyes, just in time to see the car hurtling straight for a pillar under an elevated subway. My hands tightened on the steering wheel, and I twisted it to the left.

No, I didn't want to die, I thought.

That was not God's plan for my life.

How many times had he protected me? Saved me?

I had my daughters to live for.

The car swerved, just in time to miss the pillar and avoid a deadly collision. The car rambled onto the side and I sat frozen in the front seat, sweat pouring out of my pores in buckets.

"God why me?" I screamed at the roof of the car. I pounded my fist on the steering wheel. "Don't I deserve better? I was a good wife! I've tried so hard to please Leo!"

The screaming and bawling on the side of the road continued for an hour, and suddenly, a peace like I had never experienced in my entire life came over me. There was no doubt in my mind: it was the peace that passes all understanding, the peace that God spoke of in His word.

A deep breath lifted out of my lungs, and tensions seeped from my muscles. A weak smile turned the corners of my lips and I looked at the car roof again. "Forgive me, Lord," I whispered to my Heavenly Father. "Please... give me guidance and direction. What just happened..." I swallowed, "it can't happen again. You are the Lord of my life. You are in charge of my destiny. I am a child of God, with two daughters of my own, whom you have given me charge over. This will never happen again," I told God.

And I kept my promise.

Diary Entry #8 Date: April 11, 2001

> **Deuteronomy 31:8:** *It is the Lord, who goes before you. He will be with you. He will not leave you or forsake you. Do not fear or be*

> **Isaiah 41:10:** *So do not fear, for I am with you, do not be dismayed; for I am your God. I will strengthen you and help you. I*

DIARY ENTRY #9 DATE: December 10, 2003

LORD, HAVE YOU FORGOTTEN ME?

Lord, have you forgotten me?

Remember, I called on you

To restore, resolve our marriage

I am waiting

No answer yet

Lord, have you forgotten me?

Lord, have you forgotten me?

I remember your miracles

Raised the dead, healed the blind

Lame to walk, water to wine

Lord, my need is small, I wait

Please Lord, have you forgotten me?

Lord, have you forgotten me?

How can I say that, you ask?

I have my health, my daughters, family and friends

Appeared to exude love, joy, smiles

I wait for your answer

Forgive me Lord

Lord, you have not forgotten me

Thanks!

Chapter Fourteen
Private Investigator

Enough is enough!

Over the years, and as my marriage had started to spiral, I had neglected my church attendance. My church home was in Harlem, and I used the distance as my excuse not to attend, but the truth was, all of the ups and downs of life had eroded my faith. I felt that I had been praying and believing in vain, but that was when God gave me the revelation that He hadn't forgotten me. If anything, it had been me who'd forgotten Him and wandered away. I reengaged in the fellowship and rededicated my life to God. I immersed myself in His Word and it became my lifeline. It saved me from becoming submerged by the merciless perils of life. To make things even better, I connected with a group of twelve women, who called themselves Esther's Daughters. I was full of unspeakable joy, which led me to teach adult Bible study classes and joined the dance ministry.

But Leopold's behavior continued. And like I said: enough is enough.

I was sick of his sketchy behavior, so I decided to hire a private investigator. Of course, there was no one I could tell about what I had planned. No one would understand, I was sure of it. Not even Esther's Daughters would be in a position to empathize with my situation, but they were constantly praying with me and for me. They supported me. Sometimes, very late at night, I'd pour out my heart and tell my best girlfriend, some of my problems, but there were some problems, I dare not share. Shame flooded me.

I flipped open the telephone book and scanned through the yellow pages until I found a service I thought might meet my needs. I'd tried to take this path before, but I'd chickened out. This time I wouldn't.

The conversation was brief and professional, and before I ended the call, I'd made an appointment to meet a private investigator, named Ralph, at his office. I provided him with further details and he gave me the background on his business and his experience. He had access to all manner of high-tech equipment. He also informed me that he would be available to testify in court, if necessary.

I hired him immediately, and the investigation commenced. Ralph followed Leopold day and night for an entire week, and periodically, he'd provide me with updates related to his movements. Now, all I could do was wait to see what would pan out.

"MERRY CHRISTMAS!" ONE of Esther's Daughters shouted.

"Oh, wait," another added, "don't forget, it's Gracelyn's birthday and Maryanne's birthday too!" The women cheered just as our food arrived. We were enjoying Christmas dinner, and since our birthdays fell around the same time, we'd decided to combine the celebration, but suddenly, my cell phone started to ring, and when I looked at the screen, I recognized the number as belonging to Ralph.

My chest tightened as I excused myself from the table and headed outside to take the call.

"Good evening, this is Gracelyn," I greeted him.

"Hi Mrs. Gracelyn, it's Ralph. I have an update."

The lining of my throat grew thick and I tried to swallow it away, but it was no use. "What is it?"

"Your husband is leaving the city limits," he explained. "We've been following him all day. He spent a few hours at home, and when he finally left, he was dressed up. Now he's leaving New York in his car. What would you like for me to do?"

There was only thing for him to do. "Follow him," I barked the order.

"Of course," he agreed. "Just so you're aware, to follow him outside of the jurisdiction will be an increase in fees. Is that okay with you?"

"Do it!" Without saying anything more, I ended the phone call and returned inside to continue the celebration.

The next day, I met Ralph at a local McDonald's. At that time he gave me the evidence he'd collected during his investigation. It was a dossier full of pictures, videos and documents identifying the person Leopold had been seeing behind my back.

"What's the address of the place he went to last night?" I asked. My voice was so tight I was sure it was about to crack.

Without hesitation, Ralph gave me the information. When the meeting was done, I pulled out of the parking lot and drove directly to the address I'd been given. Under normal circumstances, I'd get lost in the mall, but my sense of direction wouldn't fail me this night.

I eased my car tires along the curb and cut off the engine. I was in a strange neighborhood on the other side of town, and I had to admit, the area was pretty nice. A smattering of houses, prefaced with manicured lawns and proverbial white fences lined the street. Now that the car lights were cut, the only illumination came from the lampposts, stationed on the sidewalk.

And the moon.

I slid down in my seat, hands still on the steering wheel, shaking like leaves fluttering in a breeze. I looked at them, and balled them into tight fists, but even that didn't make them stop.

Never would I have thought I'd be doing something like this. Never had I considered that I'd be back here, dealing with another man who had vowed to love and to cherish me, yet...

My blaring cell phone sliced into my anguished thoughts. The trill was so loud, I was certain it would wake up the entire neighborhood and alert the object of my investigation to my presence.

I shot my arm over to the passenger's seat and fished my phone out of my purse. "Lord help me," I muttered. Finally, I gripped and silenced it. Quickly, I took note of the number on the small screen. It was the private investigator, Ralph. I pressed the phone against my ear. "Hi, Ralph."

"Gracelyn, hello. I was just checking up on you to see if – "

I cut him off. "Yes, I found it," I answered. For the first time since parking, I scanned the houses in earnest. It was well past midnight, and many of the dwellings sat still and in darkness.

But there was one...

My eyes narrowed, just as an intense stinging burned the back of my eyes.

Yes, Ralph, I thought to myself. *I have found it.*

It was a green car, and *it* was parked in the back of the apartment building, next to a large, green garbage container, as if it belonged there. I'd snuck around the back of the residence, and that was when I'd seen it. Now, my eyes zipped to the house in question. The other houses were in complete darkness, but this one was lit up like a Christmas Tree.

My jaw tightened. "I've been sitting out here for almost an hour," I muttered. "It's well past midnight. I can't believe my husband would leave me alone at home for so long. He said he was out with friends. He said he'd be home. I can't believe he would – "

Ralph interrupted me. "This is a terrible situation," he said, as if confirming my innermost thoughts, "but the best thing you can do right now is to stay calm. I know you said you wanted to see it for yourself, but it would not be wise to overreact."

"Yes," I mumbled, but I didn't agree with him.

Ralph continued. "You've been collecting evidence for months, and finally, it has come down to this." He fell silent, as if waiting for me to say something, but the truth was, there was nothing I could say.

A small part of me wanted to believe that it wasn't true. Maybe this wasn't my husband's car, in this strange neighborhood, parked outside of this strange house on the other side of town. Maybe Ralph had been wrong when he reported having seen my husband in the company of another woman. There were tons of men who looked like Leopold. Could it be possible that Ralph had tracked and followed the wrong guy?

I had been through this before – two times before, to be precise. How could I have allowed it to happen again?

Suddenly, there was movement against the backdrop of the curtained window. Two silhouettes glided across like apparitions, but suddenly, they stopped. That was when I saw small arms reach up and thread around a neck; and a slender frame – one which looked entirely familiar – bent down. The ghostly shadows connected in, what I could only imagine, was a kiss.

A jolt rocked my body.

Ralph's advice, that I should stay calm, filtered through my head like a gust of wind in the treetops.

"Ralph, I have to go," I announced. Without waiting for a response, I slammed my finger against the disconnect button and glared in the direction of the quaint home. The silhouettes had relocated, and now the front door was pushing open.

I plastered my body against the car seat, trying my best not to leap through the car window, but when my eyes took in the appalling sight before me, staying calm and keeping quiet was the last thing on my mind.

Chapter Fifteen
Truth Revealed

The next morning, I awoke to Leopold staring in my face, with a loving smile on his lips.

"Happy Birthday, sweetheart." He kissed my lips, and I tried not to stiffen under his faux display of affection.

What kind of man is this? I wondered. I'd thought Kenneth was an actor, but Leopold was definitely in competition for the title. Just a few hours ago, I'd seen his car posted outside of a woman's apartment; and just a few hours ago, I'd seen the two of them together hugging and kissing. And now, he was hovering over me, as if I was the love of his life? This man was a liar and a cheat, and I wanted nothing to do with him.

But if he was an actor, then I was his co-lead. The fury I felt deep on the inside never once manifested itself on my features or in my behavior. Leopold had no clue that I knew the truth about his behavior and his indiscretions.

"It's your special day," he continued. "Let's go to dinner to celebrate; you, me, and your daughter."

I smiled. "That would be wonderful," I said. "I'd like that."

To my shock, the family evening was very enjoyable. We laughed and talked and the food was delicious; but in my mind, it was like The Last Supper. It was okay to put up a façade for now, especially because my daughter was there, but there was no way I'd let the entire night go by without saying something. I ordered the most expensive things on the menu: lobster, oysters, fish chowder. When dinner came to an end, we drove home; and just as we arrived near our apartment, my daughter asked to get out.

God is here, I thought, *because only He knows what's about to go down*.

We continued to the parking garage and I parked the car, but, did not exit. I let my eyes fall closed and asked God to be with me.

"Leopold..." my voice was soft and calm. I inhaled. "I know that you're cheating on me."

His neck jerked back, as if he were shocked by the suggestion. "Gracelyn, tell me you're not serious."

"I'm very serious, I informed him. I know what I feel." I grunted. "I know what I *know*."

Instantly, his voice transformed into a brash roar. "Why would you bring this up again, after such a great evening?" he demanded. "You know, I don't think you want to be happy with me."

"Excuse me?"

"You're always looking for something to be wrong," he clarified. "You're never satisfied."

"Leopold, perhaps you've fooled yourself into believing that you're not a lying, cheating, dog, but I know the truth."

"What are you talking about?"

Quickly and calmly, I listed off the details related to his infidelity: the woman's name, address, telephone number.

He looked at me in shock before hopping out of the car and marching for the house.

I followed in silence.

As soon as we got inside, he stomped for the bedroom and ripped out a small piece of luggage.

"What do you think you're doing?" I demanded of him.

"I'm going to my son's house," he muttered. "I don't want to stay another moment with you. All of the accusations and comments... I can't take it anymore." He pitched items into the bag and marched past.

"I am going to call your woman and let her know that I am fully aware of the fact she is having an affair with my husband," I stated calmly.

That made him freeze. "You think you know what you're talking about, Gracelyn, but you actually have no idea," he alleged. "That number you called out, it's incorrect."

"Oh is it?" I pulled out my cell phone and started dialing the number that I had committed to memory, and he stood there gawking.

After a few seconds, the woman didn't answer, but her voicemail service kicked in.

It was the next best thing.

"Hello," I started, turning away from Leopold. "You don't know me and I don't know you, but apparently we have a mutual friend: my husband. I wanted to speak with you personally to let you know that I know all about your affair with him. I also wanted to let you know that God will judge the two of you. Oh, and if you're considering it, there's no need to change your number, since I won't be calling again; but of course, if I *did* need to call, I could get your number, as I have done this time." Then I hung up.

Leopold glared at me and marched out of the door.

The following Monday, he came by to get the rest of his things. I was at home that day, but no words were spoken. In fact, he never returned.

That weekend, I took consecrated oil, which had been blessed by my Bishop and put it on the doorknob, doorbell, and all over the outside door. I did the same inside of the house. I oiled the sides of Leopold's closet door, his drawers and side of the dresser. I oiled the headboard of the bed and washed all bed linens. I cleaned out all his toiletries from the bathroom and any items on the dresser and stored

them in his closet. Then I walked through every room, seven times, in
the apartment, reciting Psalm 23:

The Lord is my Shepherd; I shall not want
He makes me to lie down in green pastures
He leads me beside the still waters.
He restores my soul; He leads me
In the paths of righteousness for His name sake.
Yea, though I walk through the valley of the shadow of death,
I will fear no evil; for thou art with me
Thy rod and thy staff, they comfort me.
Thou prepares a table before me
In the presence of my enemies
Thou anoints my head with oil, my cup runs over.
Surely, goodness and mercy shall follow me
All the days of my life
And I shall dwell
In the house of the LORD FOREVER!

I didn't stop there.

I hired a contractor who painted all of the rooms, bought new fur-
niture, and renovated the bathroom.

On New Year's Eve, I attended the midnight service at my church
in Harlem. We were called up to randomly select a Bible verse card
from a basket, with the hope and prayer that it would provide guidance
for the upcoming year and throughout life. When I selected my verse, I
was stunned:

Matthew 17:8
And when they had lifted up their eyes, they saw no man, save Jesus only.

Immediately, I substituted 'they' for Gracelyn, and 'man' for
Leopold. I personalized the verse. Now the verse read:
"And when Gracelyn had lifted up her eyes, she saw no Leopold, save Jesus
only."

Tears of joy filled my eyes. God had it under control. The secrets, shame, and shackles, they were no more. I was a new woman. That day, my life changed for the very best. I had been redeemed.

Chapter Sixteen
Jesus, Jesus!

Reverend Joel Osteen was at Madison Square Garden in Manhattan, and there was no way I was going to miss the opportunity to attend such a dynamic evening. I needed the refueling. Now that I had drawn so close to God, I took advantage of every opportunity to be in His presence and learn more about His Word, and how I could apply it to my life. God was my lifeline, and I knew that without Him, I wouldn't survive.

I left my car at home and walked my way to the grand arena. There were hordes of people and the atmosphere was dynamic. It was a riveting and exhilarating experience, and I left at twelve-thirty in the morning, completely revived. Quickly, I made my way to the subway and got off at the stop closest to my home, then I continued to walk.

As I reached the pathway to my apartment, I noticed three teenagers walking towards me. They were wearing dark clothes, and hoods had been tugged over their heads.

I hastened my footsteps and wrapped my hand over the strap of my purse. After what had happened when I was going to Columbia University many years ago, I was completely alert, and anxiety snaked around me.

Soon, one of the teenagers walked alongside me, while the other two lagged behind. It wasn't long before I realized I was surrounded.

Suddenly, one of the boys snatched my purse and bolted away. Quickly, I burst into a full-out sprint and chased the rascal.

"Jesus! Jesus, he has my purse!" I screamed, voice ringing. My high heels dug into the pavement as I gave them chase. The fact that I had trouble with my knees didn't factor in. I was chasing down the little mugger, and there was little that was going to stop me!

The boy dashed across a median.

I ran across the median.

He ran across the grass, and I followed shouting to the top of my lungs. "Jesus! Jesus, stop that boy!"

With agility, he sprinted across the road, but I wasn't far behind shouting,

"Jesus, Jesus!"

In fact, the boy was never out of my sight.

Just then, a group of security men who were working the nightshift at the apartment complex heard the commotion and came running. Quickly, one man gripped the boy, who was still clutching my purse, they saw the teenager with my purse and jerked him to a halt by the collar of his shirt.

The other boys dashed away, but not before looking over their shoulders.

Finally, I caught up, both exhausted and furious. I stomped into his face. "I was downtown at Madison Square Garden, praising my Lord and you have me running all over Parkchester at one o'clock in the morning!" My voice was a seething whisper. I paused, secretly trying to catch my breath. "I should slap you!"

"Now, don't do that, ma'am," the security man advised. "We're already going to press charges on this young man. We don't want to have to add assault charges for you too."

We completed paperwork, and I watched as they thrust the young boy into a waiting police car and rushed him away.

When the commotion had died down, one of the security men who'd assisted offered to walk me back to my apartment. When he noticed the distance, he chuckled. "Ma'am, you almost ran a marathon," he joked, trying to lighten the tension.

I laughed, glad for the joke and the reprieve. "I was going to get my purse by hook or by crook," I replied. "There was no way I was going to let that young man get away with what he'd tried to do."

When I arrived at my home, my youngest daughter was outside waiting. A worried expression marked her features.

"Mom!" She dashed into my arms and we embraced in a tight hug and I squeezed her. "Oh my gosh, Mom, is everything okay? You called when you left Madison Square Garden and I was sure you would have been home before then." She cast her eyes on the security officer.

"Your mother is just fine," he reassured her, smiling. "She's a true fighter, for sure."

We chuckled together, but my daughter was still unsure.

I pulled her into another hug. "The kind gentleman is right, sweetheart," I confirmed.

"Well, you're safe and sound now," he stated as he turned to leave. "We'll call you when we need you to testify in court. In the meantime, if you have any questions, call the police station."

In two weeks, I appeared in court to testify about the experience, and the judge and jurors laughed in amusement. As I relayed the details.

The judge stroked his beard and stared at the boy whose head was hung in shame. "Miss Love, what do you think we should do with this young man?" he asked.

I stared at him. He was a child, I thought, and my heart was for children. Still, this boy had chosen a destructive path and he needed to learn a valuable lesson. Suddenly, thoughts of the lessons I'd learned over the years rushed me. I thought about God's love and his redemption. I'd made mistakes and I'd learned lessons.

That was what this young man needed.

I narrowed my eyes at him. "Send him to a seniors' home and let him empty bed pens," I suggested.

The room erupted in laughter.

The judge picked up his gavel and slammed it on the docket. "So said, so done!"

Chapter Seventeen
Retirement

I divorced Leopold and had a new outlook on life. I spoke to God and asked Him to forgive me for not succeeding in this marriage. I really wanted this marriage to work. I loved my husband. I forgave my third husband, even though he never knew until years later. Now, I was thriving and flourishing. Where I had depended on men to fulfill me, I now knew that the only true fulfillment came from my relationship with my Savior. I refocused and redirected my energy towards my daughters and their growing families.

Matthew 18:21
Then Peter came to Him and said, Lord, how often shall my brother sin against me and I forgive him? Jesus said unto him, I say unto thee, until seven times: but, until seventy times seven.

The following year in 2010, after twenty-eight years of teaching, I retired from the New York City, Board of Education. It was an early retirement, so I wouldn't receive a full pension, but I was not at all anxious about my decision. Family was more important to me, and I knew that God had it all under control.

My older daughter's family moved to Texas, and whenever I visited, my only grandchild was growing like a beanstalk. I was desperate to see him grow up, so the decision to move to Texas was an easy one. I purchased a beautiful two-bedroom home in the suburbs, near my daughter's home and home schooled my four-year-old grandson for a year.

When it was time for him to enter kindergarten class, I volunteered in his class twice a week.

Diary Entry#10 Date: May 20, 2014

<u>**NOT GROUNDED**</u>

Ironically, I think

Born, Fed, Raised

In Bermuda

But I feel like

A Stranger

Not Grounded

A Wanderer

A Drifter

Looking for Security

A Sanctuary

A Surety

But I feel like

An Emigrant

An Intruder

Not Grounded

Not Established

Not Settled

But then, I am reminded

What the Bible said

> **Ephesians 3:17**
>
> *So that Christ may dwell in your hearts through faith. And I pray that you are being rooted and established in love.*

AFTER SOME TIME, MY daughter's family decided to move back to Bermuda. I was surprised, disappointed, and unsure. I'd found a wonderful church home and developed close

relationships with my neighbors. Not only that, I'd always asserted that I would never go back

to Bermuda to live.

Never, say never!

They say there's nothing new under the sun, and I agree. Life appears to be one big circle. I arrived, feeling the weight of anxiety; anticipating the stares and pointing fingers of judgement, but friends and family received me with open arms. They were so glad to see me back in the island. To my shock and pleasure, my life in Bermuda was good. I enjoyed my immediate family and my extended family. It was great to experience some of Bermuda's traditions again, like Bermuda Cassava Pie, potato salad, and the famous codfish and potato breakfast. On specific holidays the sounds of the Gombeys would ring through the streets, and crowds of islanders would trail behind them like ants, chanting and singing. It was remarkable to be awakened, in the morning, by birds chirping, then gaze at the calm, clear, blue ocean. The island exuded peacefulness and tranquility.

I purchased a little red car to drive around on Bermuda's narrow, curvy streets. When you come around the corners, driving on the left side, it appears that you may end up in the Atlantic Ocean. Driving in Bermuda, requires nerves of steel.

I became a member of The First Church of God, a Pentecostal Church. Bishop's teaching and preaching provoked me to be a true disciple and worshipper of the Lord. I listened intently to his preaching and examined myself. Often, I'd cringe and wince at my past. I realized that I didn't like myself. Shame engulfed me. Secrets imprisoned me. Shackles constricted me. I felt unworthy of God's love. Tears flowed, uncontrollably, down my cheeks. I hung my head in humiliation. I felt ashamed, mortified before God. I asked Him for forgiveness and knew that He did forgive me. Then, I smiled and rejoiced, because in my heart, I knew that this was all that mattered.

Diary Entry #11 Date: June 23, 2016

<u>**BERMUDA'S BEAUTY**</u>

As I gaze upon BERMUDA'S BEAUTY
From Earth to Heaven
There's Love showered from God
The cottony, fluffy clouds float
Ever so quietly, gently
Not rushing, caressing the sky
The hues of blues
Reflecting the ocean vastness
Sun shines ever so brightly
SMILING AT BERMUDA'S BEAUTY
The flora, the flowers, the plants
Reveal God's love
Smiling upward to Heaven
Fragrant perfumes mist the air
Trees, green, stately swaying
In the gentle sea breeze
CARESSING BERMUDA'S BEAUTY
Cardinals, Sparrows, Chickadees
Flutter TO and FRO
Dogs, cats, frogs,
Running, scampering, jumping
Yelping, caterwauling
REJOICING IN BERMUDA'S BEAUTY
Bermudians rushing here and there
Some stop to greet their fellow man

People hurting, People crucifying

Grief, gloom grips their aching hearts

UNAWARE OF BERMUDA'S BEAUTY

Lord, I cry out, stop them

Open their eyes, hearts

Take time, to smell the roses

Walk down memory lane

Hug a friend, call a buddy

APPRECIATE BERMUDA'S BEAUTY

God said in His Word

If you go to the Heavens

You, Lord are there

You said, If I lie down

In the deepest part of the earth

You, Lord are there

In darkness, in light

You, Lord are there

Lord, I see you

IN BERMUDA'S BEAUTY!

Genesis 1:11

And God said, Let the earth bring forth grass, the herb yielding seed, and the fruit tree yielding fruit after his kind, whose seed is in itself, upon the earth: and it was so.

Genesis 1:20

And God said, Let the waters bring forth abundantly the moving creature that hath life, and fowl that may fly above the earth in the open firmament of heaven.

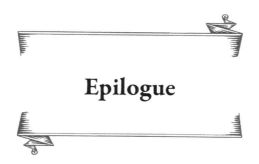

Epilogue

This is my story. It's transparent, candid, and objective. Reflecting on my life, I could say I wished I'd made better choices, or listened to God, or asked God first, but I didn't, as a result, I suffered emotionally, mentally, spiritually, and also physically.

I don't have the right to blame others for my misfortunes and my unfortunate circumstances. I am to blame. I had choices. I chose my destiny, instead of allowing God to direct my path. In Proverbs 3:6, *"In all thy ways acknowledge Him, and He will direct thy path."* But, I did not listen and obey God. I chose to do what I wanted to do. Therefore, I had to suffer the consequences of my disobedience. But than God says, 1 John1:9, *"If we confess our sins, he is faithful and just and will forgive our sins."* I confessed my sins and God forgave. me. God loves me, and I know this because I AM HERE! The Bible says, *"For God so loved the world that He gave His only Son, that whosoever believeth in Him, shall not perish but have everlasting life."*

In conclusion, I thank God, and give Him all the glory, honor and praise. Jesus died for my sins and was resurrected from the dead. He lives.

I wrote my story to inform my readers that God is alive and He is a forgiving God. No matter how far away you have travelled from God, He is still there waiting for you to call His name and ask for forgiveness. He will embrace you with love, grace, and mercy. My secrets, shame, and shackles imprisoned me for years. One night, early in the morning, kneeling at my bedside, unable to bear my burdens, floods of tears cascading down my tearstained, rosy cheeks, my soul cried out with agonizing screams, "Forgive me Lord, for I have sinned again. Forgive me Lord, for I have sinned again!" Exhaustion gripped my body and I collapsed on the floor, whimpering, "God forgive me please."

God said, *"Come to me, all you are weary and burdened, and I will give you rest."*

I DID!

Diary Entry#12 Date: November 16, 2018

Psalm 86:5

For you Lord, are good, and ready to forgive. And abundant in loving kindness to all who call upon you.

Ephesians 4:32

Be kind to one another, tenderhearted, forgiving one another, as God in Christ forgave you.

Jeremiah 29:11

For I know the plans I have for you, declares the Lord, plans to prosper you and not to harm you, plans to give hope and future.

Deuteronomy 31:6

Be strong and courageous. Do not be afraid or terrified because of them, for the Lord your God goes with you, He will never leave you nor forsake you.

DIARY ENTRY#13 DATE: July 7, 2018

<u>JUST GOD! GOD SAYS</u>

Just God! God says
Don't look to the right,
Nor to the left
Don't travel the road, wide
Journey the narrow and straight
Look to me!
I'm here! says God
No one else is near
Just God! God says
Problems come, failures rage
Both day and night
Throws me for a loop, a spin
Try to figure out a solution
Look to me!
I'm here! says God
No one else is near
Just God! God says
Cast your burdens, fears
On me, God says
Your cares, anxieties are mine
Lighten your heavy load
Look to me
I'm here! says God
No one is near
Just God! Says God
Happiness, pleasures overflow
Laughter, mirth explodes
Love, friendship propels affection
Peace, tranquility, joy, bliss throughout
Look to me
I'm here! says God
No one is near
Just God! God says
YES! JUST GOD!
GOD IS ENOUGH!

About the Author

Gracelyn Love Lillamay Davis is an outgoing, friendly, woman, whose Bermuda smile invites anyone to stop and chat with her. Gracelyn loves her two beautiful, smart, loving daughters very much and is extremely proud of them. But, her only grandchild, a grandson, is the one she talks mostly about, lovingly and proudly, all the time. Gracelyn appears to be filled with an overflow of joy. Her love for teaching children and adults is emanated through the cheerfulness and glow on her face. She is so happy to be in the presence of God and openly worships and exalts His name without hesitation. Her favorite Book of the Bible is Psalm 121. I will lift my eyes unto the hills, from whence cometh my help. My help cometh from the Lord, which made heaven and earth. She reads this Psalm every day. This Psalm sustained her and gave her hope. Her favorite Scripture verse is Isaiah 40:31. But they that wait upon the Lord shall renew their strength; they shall mount up with wings as eagles; they shall run, and not be weary; and they shall walk, and not faint. God was her strength through all her trials, ordeals and pain.

Though there were times, that she may not have acknowledged God's presence, but in the end, she realized God was always there through her Secrets, Shame, Shackles. Her early Biblical teachings facilitated strongly in bringing her back to God. Frequently, she is back in Bermuda, visiting. Welcome back Island Girl!

Made in the
USA
Lexington, KY